ADVOCACY

Lord Pannick celebrates advocacy: that controversial legal issues are decided in court after reasoned argument in which the participants refrain (usually) from shouting, personal insults or threats, and the points on each side of the debate are tested for their relevance, their accuracy, and their strength. The book seeks to identify the central characteristics of good and bad advocacy with the aid of examples from courtrooms in the UK and abroad. Lord Pannick also examines the morality of advocacy – that the advocate sets out views to which he does not necessarily subscribe, on behalf of clients for whom she may feel admiration, indifference or contempt. Lord Pannick seeks to answer the question he is often asked – more by friends than by judges – "How can you act for such terrible people?" Finally, he addresses the future of advocacy, arguing it should and will survive pressures for efficiency and technological developments.

LORD DAVID PANNICK KC has been a practising barrister since 1980. His most famous case was arguing for Gina Miller in persuading the Supreme Court that it was unlawful for Prime Minister Boris Johnson to advise the Queen to suspend parliament in 2019 because of his wish to "get Brexit done". Lord Pannick has appeared in more than 125 cases in the Supreme Court and its predecessor the Appellate Committee of the House of Lords. He is also a crossbench member of the House of Lords and a Fellow of All Souls College, Oxford.

ADVOCACY

LORD DAVID PANNICK KC

Blackstone Chambers
Fellow of All Souls College, Oxford
Crossbench Peer in the House of Lords

CAMBRIDGE
UNIVERSITY PRESS

CAMBRIDGE
UNIVERSITY PRESS

Shaftesbury Road, Cambridge CB2 8EA, United Kingdom

One Liberty Plaza, 20th Floor, New York, NY 10006, USA

477 Williamstown Road, Port Melbourne, VIC 3207, Australia

314–321, 3rd Floor, Plot 3, Splendor Forum, Jasola District Centre, New Delhi – 110025, India

103 Penang Road, #05–06/07, Visioncrest Commercial, Singapore 238467

Cambridge University Press is part of Cambridge University Press & Assessment, a department of the University of Cambridge.

We share the University's mission to contribute to society through the pursuit of education, learning and research at the highest international levels of excellence.

www.cambridge.org
Information on this title: www.cambridge.org/9781009338103

DOI: 10.1017/9781009338097

First published 2023

A catalogue record for this publication is available from the British Library

Library of Congress Cataloging-in-Publication Data
NAMES: Pannick, David, author.
TITLE: Advocacy / Lord David Pannick KC, Blackstone Chambers, Fellow of All Souls College, Oxford, Crossbench Peer in the House of Lords.
DESCRIPTION: First edition. | New York, NY : Cambridge University Press, 2023. | SERIES: Haml the hamlyn lectures | Includes bibliographical references and index.
IDENTIFIERS: LCCN 2022046579 (print) | LCCN 2022046580 (ebook) | ISBN 9781009338103 (hardback) | ISBN 9781009338110 (paperback) | ISBN 9781009338097 (epub)
SUBJECTS: LCSH: Practice of law–Great Britain. | Practice of law–Moral and ethical aspects–Great Britain. | Lawyers–Great Britain.
CLASSIFICATION: LCC KD460 .P33 2023 (print) | LCC KD460 (ebook) | DDC 340.023/41–dc23/eng/20230103
LC record available at https://lccn.loc.gov/2022046579
LC ebook record available at https://lccn.loc.gov/2022046580

ISBN 978-1-009-33810-3 Hardback

To Nathalie

CONTENTS

The Hamlyn Trust owes its existence today to the will of the late Miss Emma Warburton Hamlyn of Torquay, who died in 1941 at the age of eighty. She came of an old and well-known Devon family. Her father, William Bussell Hamlyn, practised in Torquay as a solicitor and JP for many years, and it seems likely that Miss Hamlyn founded the trust in his memory. Emma Hamlyn was a woman of strong character, intelligent and cultured, well-versed in literature, music and art, and a lover of her country. She travelled extensively in Europe and Egypt, and apparently took considerable interest in the law and ethnology of the countries and cultures that she visited. An account of Miss Hamlyn by Professor Chantal Stebbings of the University of Exeter may be found, under the title "The Hamlyn Legacy", in volume 42 of the published lectures.

Miss Hamlyn bequeathed the residue of her estate on trust in terms which it seems were her own. The wording was thought to be vague, and the will was taken to the Chancery Division of the High Court, which in November 1948 approved a Scheme for the administration of the trust. Paragraph 3 of the Scheme, which follows Miss Hamlyn's own wording, is as follows:

> The object of the charity is the furtherance by lectures or otherwise among the Common People of the United Kingdom of Great Britain and Northern Ireland of the

Hamlyn Seminar, normally held at the Institute of Advanced Legal Studies in the University of London, to mark the publication of the Lectures in printed book form. The Trustees have also, from time to time, provided financial support for a variety of projects which, in various ways, have disseminated knowledge or have promoted a wider public understanding of the law.

This, the seventy-second series of lectures, was delivered by Lord David Pannick KC at Grays Inn Hall, London, the Senedd Building, Cardiff, and the Gulbenkian Theatre at the University of Oxford. The Board of Trustees would like to record its appreciation to David Pannick and also to the three institutions which generously hosted these Lectures.

Avrom Sherr
Chair of the Trustees

> knowledge of the Comparative Jurisprudence and Ethnology of the Chief European countries including the United Kingdom, and the circumstances of the growth of such jurisprudence to the Intent that the Common People of the United Kingdom may realise the privileges which in law and custom they enjoy in comparison with other European Peoples and realising and appreciating such privileges may recognise the responsibilities and obligations attaching to them.

At present there are eight Trustees:

From the outset it was decided that the objects of the Trust could be best achieved by means of an annual course of public lectures of outstanding interest and quality by eminent lecturers, and by their subsequent publication and distribution to a wider audience. The first of the Lectures were delivered by the Rt Hon. Lord Justice Denning (as he then was) in 1949. Since then there has been an unbroken series of annual Lectures published until 2005 by Sweet & Maxwell and from 2006 by Cambridge University Press. A complete list of the Lectures may be found on pages xi–xv. In 2005 the Trustees decided to supplement the Lectures with an annual

THE HAMLYN TRUST

The Hamlyn Trust owes its existence today to the will of the late Miss Emma Warburton Hamlyn of Torquay, who died in 1941 at the age of eighty. She came of an old and well-known Devon family. Her father, William Bussell Hamlyn, practised in Torquay as a solicitor and JP for many years, and it seems likely that Miss Hamlyn founded the trust in his memory. Emma Hamlyn was a woman of strong character, intelligent and cultured, well-versed in literature, music and art, and a lover of her country. She travelled extensively in Europe and Egypt, and apparently took considerable interest in the law and ethnology of the countries and cultures that she visited. An account of Miss Hamlyn by Professor Chantal Stebbings of the University of Exeter may be found, under the title "The Hamlyn Legacy", in volume 42 of the published lectures.

Miss Hamlyn bequeathed the residue of her estate on trust in terms which it seems were her own. The wording was thought to be vague, and the will was taken to the Chancery Division of the High Court, which in November 1948 approved a Scheme for the administration of the trust. Paragraph 3 of the Scheme, which follows Miss Hamlyn's own wording, is as follows:

> The object of the charity is the furtherance by lectures or otherwise among the Common People of the United Kingdom of Great Britain and Northern Ireland of the

CONTENTS

To Nathalie

CAMBRIDGE
UNIVERSITY PRESS

Shaftesbury Road, Cambridge CB2 8EA, United Kingdom

One Liberty Plaza, 20th Floor, New York, NY 10006, USA

477 Williamstown Road, Port Melbourne, VIC 3207, Australia

314–321, 3rd Floor, Plot 3, Splendor Forum, Jasola District Centre, New Delhi – 110025, India

103 Penang Road, #05–06/07, Visioncrest Commercial, Singapore 238467

Cambridge University Press is part of Cambridge University Press & Assessment, a department of the University of Cambridge.

We share the University's mission to contribute to society through the pursuit of education, learning and research at the highest international levels of excellence.

www.cambridge.org
Information on this title: www.cambridge.org/9781009338103

DOI: 10.1017/9781009338097

First published 2023

A catalogue record for this publication is available from the British Library

Library of Congress Cataloging-in-Publication Data
NAMES: Pannick, David, author.
TITLE: Advocacy / Lord David Pannick KC, Blackstone Chambers, Fellow of All Souls College, Oxford, Crossbench Peer in the House of Lords.
DESCRIPTION: First edition. | New York, NY : Cambridge University Press, 2023. | SERIES: Haml the hamlyn lectures | Includes bibliographical references and index.
IDENTIFIERS: LCCN 2022046579 (print) | LCCN 2022046580 (ebook) | ISBN 9781009338103 (hardback) | ISBN 9781009338110 (paperback) | ISBN 9781009338097 (epub)
SUBJECTS: LCSH: Practice of law–Great Britain. | Practice of law–Moral and ethical aspects–Great Britain. | Lawyers–Great Britain.
CLASSIFICATION: LCC KD460 .P33 2023 (print) | LCC KD460 (ebook) | DDC 340.023/41–dc23/eng/20230103
LC record available at https://lccn.loc.gov/2022046579
LC ebook record available at https://lccn.loc.gov/2022046580

ISBN 978-1-009-33810-3 Hardback

ADVOCACY

LORD DAVID PANNICK KC

Blackstone Chambers
Fellow of All Souls College, Oxford
Crossbench Peer in the House of Lords

CAMBRIDGE
UNIVERSITY PRESS

1949 Freedom under the Law by the Rt Hon. Lord Denning
1950 The Inheritance of the Common Law by Richard O'Sullivan
1951 The Rational Strength of English Law by Professor F. H. Lawson
1952 English Law and the Moral Law by Professor A. L. Goodhart
1953 The Queen's Peace by Sir Carleton Kemp Allen
1954 Executive Discretion and Judicial Control by Professor C. J. Hamson
1955 The Proof of Guilt by Professor Glanville Williams
1956 Trial by Jury by the Rt Hon. Lord Devlin
1957 Protection from Power under English Law by the Rt Hon. Lord MacDermott
1958 The Sanctity of Contracts in English Law by Professor Sir David Hughes Parry
1959 Judge and Jurist in the Reign of Victoria by C. H. S. Fifoot
1960 The Common Law in India by M. C. Setalvad
1961 British Justice: The Scottish Contribution by Professor Sir Thomas Smith
1962 Lawyer and Litigant in England by the Rt Hon. Sir Robert Megarry
1963 Crime and the Criminal Law by the Baroness Wootton of Abinger

1964	Law and Lawyers in the United States by Dean Erwin N. Griswold
1965	New Law for a New World? by the Rt Hon. Lord Tangley
1966	Other People's Law by the Rt Hon. Lord Kilbrandon
1967	The Contribution of English Law to South African Law: and the Rule of Law in South Africa by the Hon. O. D. Schreiner
1968	Justice in the Welfare State by Professor H. Street
1969	The British Tradition in Canadian Law by the Hon. Bora Laskin
1970	The English Judge by Henry Cecil
1971	Punishment, Prison and the Public by Professor Sir Rupert Cross
1972	Labour and the Law by Professor Sir Otto Kahn-Freund
1973	Maladministration and Its Remedies by Sir Kenneth Wheare
1974	English Law – the New Dimension by the Rt Hon. Lord Scarman
1975	The Land and the Development; or, The Turmoil and the Torment by Sir Desmond Heap
1976	The National Insurance Commissioners by Sir Robert Micklethwait
1977	The European Communities and the Rule of Law by Lord Mackenzie Stuart
1978	Liberty, Law and Justice by Professor Sir Norman Anderson
1979	Social History and Law Reform by Professor Lord McGregor of Durris
1980	Constitutional Fundamentals by Professor Sir William Wade

1981 Intolerable Inquisition? Reflections on the Law of Tax by Hubert Monroe

1982 The Quest for Security: Employees, Tenants, Wives by Professor Tony Honoré

1983 Hamlyn Revisited: The British Legal System Today by Lord Hailsham of St Marylebone

1984 The Development of Consumer Law and Policy – Bold Spirits and Timorous Souls by Sir Gordon Borrie

1985 Law and Order by Professor Ralf Dahrendorf

1986 The Fabric of English Civil Justice by Sir Jack Jacob

1987 Pragmatism and Theory in English Law by Professor P. S. Atiyah

1988 Justification and Excuse in the Criminal Law by Professor J. C. Smith

1989 Protection of the Public – A New Challenge by the Rt Hon. Lord Justice Woolf

1990 The United Kingdom and Human Rights by Dr Claire Palley

1991 Introducing a European Legal Order by Gordon Slynn

1992 Speech and Respect by Professor Richard Abel

1993 The Administration of Justice by Lord Mackay of Clashfern

1994 Blackstone's Tower: The English Law School by Professor William Twining

1995 From the Test Tube to the Coffin: Choice and Regulation in Private Life by the Hon. Mrs Justice Hale

1996 Turning Points of the Common Law by the Rt Hon. the Lord Cooke of Thorndon

1997 Commercial Law in the Next Millennium by Professor Roy Goode

1998 Freedom, Law and Justice by the Rt Hon. Lord Justice Sedley

1999 The State of Justice by Professor Michael Zander QC

2000 Does the United Kingdom Still Have a Constitution? by Professor Anthony King

2001 Human Rights, Serious Crime and Criminal Procedure by Professor Andrew Ashworth QC

2002 Legal Conundrums in Our Brave New World by Baroness Kennedy of the Shaws

2003 Judicial Activism by the Hon. Justice Michael Kirby AC CMG

2004 Rights at Work: Global, European and British Perspectives by Sir Bob Hepple QC, FBA

2005 Can Human Rights Survive? by Professor Conor Gearty

2006 The Sovereignty of Law: The European Way by Sir Francis Jacobs KCMG, QC

2007 The Prisoners' Dilemma by Professor Nicola Lacey

2008 Judging Civil Justice by Dame Hazel Genn

2009 Widening Horizons: The Influence of Comparative Law and International Law on Domestic Law by Lord Bingham

2010 Lawyers and the Public Good: Democracy in Action? by Alan Paterson

2011 The Rule of Law and the Measure of Property by Jeremy Waldron

2012 Aspects of Law Reform: An Insider's Perspective by Jack Straw

2013 The Common Law Constitution by Sir John Laws

2014 UK, EU and Global Administrative Law by Paul Craig

2015 A "Magna Carta" for Children? – Rethinking Children's Rights by Professor Michael Freeman

2016 Fairness in Criminal Justice: Golden Threads and Pragmatic Patches by Dame Sian Elias

2017 Thinking about Statutes: Interpretation, Interaction, Improvement by Professor Andrew Burrows QC

2018 Making Comparisons in Equality Law by Robin Allen

2019 English Law under Two Elizabeths by Sir John Baker

PREFACE AND ACKNOWLEDGEMENTS

The three chapters of this book are expanded versions of the Hamlyn Lectures 2021. I gave the lectures on 9 November 2021 in Gray's Inn Hall, London, on 10 November 2021 in the Senedd Building, Cardiff, and on 11 November 2021 in the Gulbenkian Lecture Theatre in the St Cross Building, Oxford. There was also a very large remote audience watching and listening online.

I have added some references to developments after the delivery of the Lectures.

I am very grateful to Avrom Sherr, the Chair of the Hamlyn Trustees, for inviting me to give these Lectures and for his patience, good humour and organisational skills.

A number of friends and colleagues commented on drafts of the Lectures, pointing out some of my errors, exaggerations and stupidities. None of them is responsible for those that remain. Thank you, in particular, to Michael Beloff, Abraham Chan, Jeffrey Elkinson, Cécile Fabre, Bryan Garner, Tony Grabiner, Guy Pratte, Joshua Rozenberg and Richard Susskind.

Thank you for all their help in bringing this book to publication to Tom Randall and Claire Sissen of Cambridge University Press, to Vinithan Sedumadhavan (Project Manager at Straive) and to Joan Dale Lace (for her copy-editing skills).

I have on my desk the copy of Sir Malcolm Hilbery's *Duty and Art in Advocacy* (1959, written in 1946) presented to me by Leonard Caplan QC, the Treasurer of Gray's Inn, on my call to the Bar on 26 July 1979. I shall be very disappointed if my lectures are not more stimulating and entertaining for students, lawyers and others interested in advocacy.

1

The Essence of Advocacy

During oral argument in the United States Supreme Court in an important constitutional case in 1972, Mr Justice Douglas asked the assistant prosecutor from Louisville, Kentucky why his submissions had failed to address the leading cases. "Your Honor must realise", the advocate replied, "I am a very busy man."[1]

In my forty years – so far – as a busy advocate, I have been thinking about advocacy, bad as well as good, its morality and its future. So I am delighted that the Hamlyn Trustees gave me the opportunity to develop my thoughts in three lectures. Especially as, in more than seventy years of Hamlyn Lectures, very little has been said on a subject so central to justice and the rule of law.[2]

In 1941, Miss Emma Warburton Hamlyn of Torquay died leaving money on trust for lectures "among the Common People of the United Kingdom of Great Britain and Northern

[1] *Branzburg* v *Hayes* 408 US 665 (1972). See Floyd Abrams *Speech to Graduating Class, University of Michigan Law School* (13 May 1990), pp. 3–4.

[2] The subject was mentioned by R E Megarry *Lawyer and Litigant in England* (1962), chapter 2, and by Erwin N Griswold *Law and Lawyers in the United States* (1965), chapter 2. And, as my former pupil master Michael Beloff QC has pointed out to me, one of the star advocates in the television series *LA Law* (eight seasons from 1986), Michael Kuzak, was played by the actor Harry Hamlin (no relation).

Ireland" so that they "may realise the privileges which in law and custom they enjoy in comparison with other European Peoples", a trust purpose particularly relevant post-Brexit. One of those privileges is that oral advocacy has a central place in our legal system, by comparison with continental legal systems, as anyone who has appeared in, or watched the proceedings of, the Court of Justice of the EU or the European Court of Human Rights will confirm.

After Lord Justice Denning published a book based on the first set of Hamlyn Lectures, *Freedom Under the Law*, in 1949, the Lord Chancellor's Department produced a list of his "errors".[3] I hope to provoke a more positive response from all those interested in the law.

There is a danger in lecturing on advocacy: what you say may be wholly unpersuasive. Especially as, according to Quintilian in the first century AD, "[t]he art of speaking depends on much effort, continual study, varied kinds of exercise, long experience, profound wisdom and unfailing strategic sense".[4] The importance of the subject justifies the risk that these lectures may fail to convince.

We should celebrate the concept of advocacy: that legal issues in civil and criminal courts are decided after reasoned argument in which the participants refrain (usually)

[3] The Lord Chancellor, Lord Jowitt, also wrote to Lord Justice Denning to remind him that the less judges said out of court "the better". See R F V Heuston *Lives of the Lord Chancellors 1940–1970* (1987), p. 214 and Robert Stevens *The Independence of the Judiciary: The View from the Lord Chancellor's Office* (1993), p. 93.

[4] Quintilian *The Orator's Education*, Book 2, chapter 13 (edited and translated by Donald A Russell, 2001), p. 347.

from shouting, personal insults or threats, and the points on each side of the debate are tested for their relevance, their accuracy and their strength by an independent adjudicator.[5] Such a process does not guarantee that the correct answer will be achieved. But it does make such a conclusion more likely, and it also means that the parties whose arguments do not prevail are more willing to accept the result. I much prefer this principle to the Chinese proverb to which Jan Morris refers: that "[i]t is a step towards chaos ... when argument begins".[6]

The virtues of advocacy have force outside as well as inside the courtroom. Today, political debate increasingly involves either insulting or ignoring your opponents rather than engaging with what they say and seeking to convince people of the merits of your own position. This is not to suggest that politics should adopt legal methods of reasoning. As Lord Reed, President of the Supreme Court, said for a seven-judge panel in 2021, politics involves a very different process to adjudication. Politics concerns "the management of political disagreements within our society so as to arrive, through negotiation and compromise, and the use of the party political power obtained at democratic elections, at decisions

[5] As pointed out by James Shapiro in *Shakespeare in a Divided America* (2020), p. xxvi, one of the main reasons why Shakespeare's plays remain so relevant and powerful today is that he was "a product of an Elizabethan educational system that trained young minds to argue ... on both sides of the question". Shapiro notes at p. 89 that the young lawyer Abraham Lincoln carried around with him on circuit the works of Shakespeare.

[6] Jan Morris *Hong Kong* (2nd edition, 2000 reprint), p. 201.

whose legitimacy is accepted not because of the quality or transparency of the reasoning involved, but because of the democratic credentials of those by whom the decisions are taken".[7] Nevertheless, there is an important role for advocacy in politics: that is, seeking to persuade people of the merits of your policies and the defects of those of your opponent. In 1952, the Democratic Party nominee for President of the USA, Adlai Stevenson, said on the campaign trail that if his opponents "stop telling lies about [us], we will stop telling the truth about them".[8]

The art of persuasion is now less valued in politics, but it remains of central importance in so many forms of social discourse. We learn this at an early age: "Please can I have an ice cream?" And we exercise or experience the art of advocacy throughout our lives: from "Buy this car"[9] to "Will you marry me?"

Advocacy can be dated back at least as far as the submissions of Moses as recorded in the Old Testament. The children of Israel, freed from slavery in Egypt after God has worked miracles on their behalf, petulantly complain that Moses, their leader, has been up Mount Sinai in the presence of God for too long. They lose patience and build a golden calf

[7] *R (SC)* v *Secretary of State for Work and Pensions* [2021] 3 WLR 428 at paragraph 169.

[8] *The Yale Book of Quotations* (2006, edited by Fred R Shapiro), p. 732.

[9] See Robert B Cialdini *Influence: The Psychology of Persuasion* (1984). Note Stephen M Shapiro "Oral Argument in the Supreme Court of the United States", 33 *Catholic University Law Review* 529, 531 (1984): "Every advocate is, in an important sense, a salesperson and the object of advocacy is persuasion of other human beings."

for the purpose of idolatry. An angry God tells Moses that he intends to punish them. "But", the book of Exodus explains, "Moses set himself to placate the Lord his God." Moses, the advocate, presents some cogent and persuasive points by way of mitigation and "So the Lord relented".[10]

My subject in these lectures is oral advocacy in court – not in social discourse, politics or conversations with a deity. As Cicero pointed out in the first century BC, "no single kind of oratory suits every cause or audience or speaker or occasion".[11] Even within the legal domain, advocacy in the Supreme Court is different from advocacy in the Luton Magistrates' Court. And, as Quintilian understood, the nature of the cause will affect the style of advocacy: "What use is it to apply a lofty style to trivial causes, a concise and refined one to momentous ones; a cheerful manner to gloomy themes, a smooth one to harsh; a threatening tone when we plead for mercy, a submissive one where energy is needed, and a brutal and violent one when what the subject demands is charm?"[12]

But the basic principles of advocacy are common to all legal contexts. And they apply to whoever the advocate may be. Since the coming into force of the Courts and Legal Services Act 1990, advocacy in the High Court and above is no longer restricted to barristers. There are many solicitor

[10] *Exodus* 32:1–14. See similarly *Numbers* 14:1–21.

[11] Cicero *On the Orator* (translated by H Rackham, 1942), Book 3, chapter 54, p. 167.

[12] Quintilian *The Orator's Education*, Book 11, chapter 1 (edited and translated by Donald A Russell, 2001), p. 9.

advocates. So when I refer to "advocates" and "counsel", I of course include solicitor advocates.

In this first lecture, I want to address the essence of advocacy, though inevitably not in a comprehensive manner – Quintilian produced twelve volumes on oratory in the first century AD.

I should start by recognising that public speaking is a challenge for almost everyone. The exceptionally talented Barack Obama commented in his presidential memoirs that "[t]he days had long passed since I got nervous on a big stage".[13] The extremely self-confident Piers Morgan asserted in June 2020 that "I rarely feel any nerves before speaking in public, even if I have to wing it with no notice".[14]

For the rest of us, public speaking is a stressful experience, though perhaps not to the extent suffered by Mark Zuckerberg, the co-founder and chief executive of *Facebook*, who, it was reported in 2020, would become so worried when making presentations in public "that his PR team had to blow-dry his armpits before he went on stage".[15] Jerry Seinfeld has a stand-up comedy routine on the theme that the number one fear of the average person is public speaking. Number two is death. "How in the world is that?", asks Seinfeld. "That means to most people, if you have to go to a funeral, you would rather be in the casket than doing the eulogy."[16] Public speaking has much in common, at least in

[13] Barack Obama *A Promised Land* (2020), p. 285.

[14] Piers Morgan *The Mail on Sunday* 7 June 2020.

[15] *The Times* 20 February 2020, reporting claims (since denied) made in Steven Levy's book, *Facebook: The Inside Story* (2020).

[16] Jerry Seinfeld *Is This Anything?* (2020), p. 98.

this respect, with acting. The actress and singer Elaine Stritch suffered badly from stage fright. When she refused a drink in the wings before the start of a performance (she was a recovering alcoholic), her colleague was surprised: "You mean, you're going out there alone?"[17]

Professional advocates give speeches for a living – and almost all of us worry about what is going to happen in court. The Chief Justice of the US Supreme Court, John Roberts, said that he was always nervous appearing before that court as counsel and "if . . . you are not very nervous you don't really understand what is going on".[18] Several counsel have fainted while presenting arguments in the US Supreme Court,[19] including in 1935 Solicitor General Stanley F. Reed, who toppled over while arguing for the validity of a key piece of New Deal legislation.[20]

17 Libby Purves "Long lockdown has given us all stage fright" *The Times* 25 April 2021.

18 Clare Cushman *Courtwatchers: Eyewitness Accounts in Supreme Court History* (2011), p. 132.

19 Timothy R Johnson and Jerry Goldman *A Good Quarrel: America's Top Legal Reporters Share Stories from Inside the Supreme Court* (2009), Foreword.

20 Clare Cushman *Courtwatchers: Eyewitness Accounts in Supreme Court History* (2011), p. 130. In his recent memoirs, Graham Boal gives a very frank account of how his "stage fright" as a barrister was "almost crippling" and contributed to his alcoholism: Graham Boal *A Drink at the Bar* (2021), p. 102. And in fiction see Robert Harris *Dictator* (2015), p. 167: Cicero "was often nervous before a big oration, and suffered from loose bowels and vomiting". And John Grisham *Rogue Lawyer* (2015), p. 317: "An old trial lawyer once told me that if the day came when I walked into a courtroom and faced a jury without fear, then it was time to quit."

This is true of cases at the beginning of practice. Sir Patrick Hastings, one of the great advocates of the twentieth century, was briefed for his first case in a county court. He had prepared a cross-examination but was "too nervous to say anything. He was saved because his opponent stood up first and applied for an adjournment. 'I could have kissed him', said Hastings afterwards".[21] When Travers Humphreys conducted his first case as defence counsel early in the twentieth century, he heard nothing of what the prosecution witness said, "being engaged in a strenuous and fortunately successful effort to avoid being sick".[22]

For many barristers, however experienced and eminent, the nervousness is a permanent feature of our work. Cicero quotes the advocate Crassus, who said that "the better the orator, the more profoundly is he frightened of the difficulty of speaking, and of the doubtful fate of a speech, and of the anticipations of an audience". Crassus confessed that he would "turn pale at the outset of a speech, and quake in every limb and in all my soul".[23]

[21] H Montgomery Hyde *Sir Patrick Hastings: His Life and Cases* (1960), p. 24.

[22] Travers Humphreys *Criminal Days* (1946), p. 138.

[23] Cicero *On the Orator* (translated by E W Sutton and H Rackham, 1948), Book 1, chapter 26, p. 85. In his novel *The Last Trial* (2020), p. 11, Scott Turow expressed the effect of advocacy on his literary creation, the lawyer Sandy Stern. For nearly sixty years, Stern had approached every case "almost as if he, as much as his client, were on trial". During a case "he will sleep fitfully, as the witnesses take over his dreams". On the first day of the hearing, "anxiety was a rodent gnawing on his heart".

John Mortimer QC observed that counsel often feel "sick with anxiety before you go into court".[24] Years after giving up practice as a barrister, Mortimer wrote that he still regularly dreamt of running through the Law Courts, inappropriately dressed, to argue a case he had not prepared.[25] He described the "usual courtroom terrors" experienced by his creation, the barrister Horace Rumpole: "sweaty hands, dry mouth and a strong temptation to run out of the door and take up work as a quietly unostentatious bus conductor or lavatory attendant".[26]

Happily, the worry tends to dissipate once the case begins. A great advocate of the early twentieth century, Sir Edward Marshall Hall, "would be ill with nervousness and anxiety before he went into court, but, once there, all his anxiety would vanish".[27] And it may help advocates to keep the stress in perspective: in some foreign jurisdictions, and on occasions in this country, advocates must display real courage in taking on powerful and dangerous forces, whether an authoritarian government or malign private entities.[28]

[24] *The Times* 22 April 1992.

[25] John Mortimer *Murderers and Other Friends* (1994), p. 1. He added, at p. 11, that as leading counsel he had a junior and an instructing solicitor, "from whom I must try to hide my doubts and fears". See also Michael Beloff QC *MJBQC: A Life within and without the Law* (2022), p. 51: "This was the first but also the last time I have ever been late for court – although I continue to have recurrent nightmares about the possibility even after my retirement".

[26] John Mortimer *Rumpole and the Penge Bungalow Murders* (2004), p. 77.

[27] Edward Marjoribanks *The Life of Edward Marshall Hall* (1929), p. 178.

[28] See the comments of Judge Geoffrey Robertson QC (himself a fearless advocate) in *Prosecutor* v *Alex Brima and others* (Appeals Chamber of

To compensate for the stress, advocacy is a profession that, on the rare occasions when all goes well, gives great satisfaction to those who practise it. Cicero had experienced that there is "no more excellent thing" than the power by means of advocacy to direct a tribunal "wherever the speaker wishes, or divert them from whatever he wishes".[29] Cicero quoted the advocate Marcus Antonius as asking: "Can any music be composed that is sweeter than a well-balanced speech?"[30] Quintilian described oratory as "the best gift of the gods to man".[31]

the Special Court for Sierra Leone, 8 December 2005, concurring opinion at paragraph 78). There are also, on occasions, real risks of physical danger to counsel in this country. See "The life of a criminal defence lawyer" *The Times* 14 October 2021: "Hate mail, death threats and being spat at in the street have become part of life for Jim Sturman QC after almost 40 years at the criminal Bar."

29 Cicero *On the Orator* (translated by E W Sutton and H Rackham, 1948), Book 1, chapter 8, p. 23. Sir Sydney Kentridge QC, a great advocate approaching his 100th birthday, was asked about the secret to successful advocacy. He replied, "with a twinkle in his eye" that it helped "Having a good case to argue": *The Times* 30 June 2022.

30 Cicero *On the Orator* (translated by E W Sutton and H Rackham, 1948), Book 2, chapter 8, p. 223.

31 Quintilian *The Orator's Education*, Book 12, chapter 11 (edited and translated by Donald A Russell, 2001), p. 341. See also an equally romantic account by Richard du Cann *The Art of the Advocate* (revised edition, 1993), p. 71: "There are magical moments in all advocates' lives. To sense a response in the minds and hearts of others to the words he chooses to use and the way in which he chooses to use them is the final justification for all the dull preparation which has preceded it. It wipes away all the sacrifices he has to make and the worry and responsibility he has to bear in order to follow his calling." See also Scott Turow *Innocent* (2010), pp. 184–185: Sandy Stern's magnetism in a courtroom

I should add that there is no more dispiriting thing than returning to the clerks' room after the Court of Appeal has rejected your submissions as raising no arguable point of law. All counsel encounter unsuccessful days, and weeks, in the law. Unless you are Perry Mason, the fictional advocate in the US television series (1957–1966). He lost only 1 of 264 trials – and he won that case on appeal.[32]

It does not take much research in the law reports to find cases where even the most distinguished lawyers have had their submissions rejected in forceful terms. In 1920, Lord Birkenhead for the Judicial Committee of the Privy Council said of the argument advanced by Frederic Maugham KC, later a Lord of Appeal and Lord Chancellor, that it was "embarrassing and even ridiculous".[33] In 1947, Lord Justice Evershed rejected "a point which was born and lived and flourished and died ... in the course of Mr Beyfus' argument".[34] Lord Diplock for the Appellate Committee of the House of Lords said that the argument advanced by Mark Littman QC in a 1980 case "only requires to be stated to be

is "beyond anybody's ability to explain. He is short – barely five feet six, if that – and to be honest, pretty dumpy. You would walk past Sandy Stern on the street a thousand times. But when he stands up in court, it is as if someone lit a beacon".

32 See *American Bar Association Journal* (1994), p. 35. A more realistic representation of the life of the advocate is in Scott Turow's *The Last Trial* (2020), p. 371: "Losing, even when you know it's coming, is always painful. As [another lawyer] once said to Stern, 'Let's face it, Sandy. You're never really ready to get kicked in the balls'."

33 *McCawley* v *The King* [1920] AC 691, 705.

34 *Greenhalgh* v *Mallard* [1947] 2 All ER 255, 259.

rejected".[35] In 1982, Mr Justice Nourse commented that "Sir John [Foster QC] said that this is a point not covered by authority. My respectful answer to that is that, but for this case, I would have doubted that it was a point for which authority was needed".[36] The advocacy skills of my colleague Sir James Eadie KC have ensured that the case for the government has been presented as attractively and persuasively as possible over the past decade. But even he has had an argument rejected by Lord Wilson for the Supreme Court as being "misplaced even at the high level of pedantry on which it has been set".[37] And he has been compared by Lord Reed for the Supreme Court to "the Fat Boy in *The Pickwick Papers*", in that "he sought to make our flesh creep".[38]

[35] *Lonrho Ltd* v *Shell Petroleum Co Ltd* [1980] 1 WLR 627, 635. Other examples of advocacy unceremoniously rejected by the court include *Pointing* v *Wilson* [1927] 1 KB 382, 384, where Lord Chief Justice Hewart said that the argument of counsel amounted to a "desperate proposition". In *R* v *Knights* [2006] 1 AC 368, paragraph 26, Lord Brown for the Appellate Committee of the House of Lords observed that "None of the remaining arguments which Mr Glen optimistically sought to urge upon your Lordships are to my mind worthy even of separate mention". In *Ali* v *Secretary of State for the Home Department* [1994] Imm AR 69, 76, Lord Justice Scott, for the Court of Appeal, said: "It is no part of the function of the Court of Appeal or indeed of any court to treat with respect an argument which deserves none. In the present appeal the argument that has been put before the court on behalf of the appellant is as hopeless as any argument can ever be."

[36] *Inland Revenue Commissioners* v *Duchess of Portland* [1982] Ch 314, 320.

[37] *Mandalia* v *Secretary of State for the Home Department* [2015] 1 WLR 4546, paragraph 23.

[38] *Cox* v *Ministry of Justice* [2016] AC 660, paragraph 43.

I keep close to hand at all times a cathartic collection of cuttings about advocates whose advocacy was unappealing. It is reassuring to bear in mind that your own performance could always have been so much worse. After a bad day in court, I remind myself that Edward Kenealy, leading counsel in 1873 for the Tichborne claimant, conducted the case "in a manner so violent, and to himself so disastrous, that his mind may almost be supposed to have become unsettled in the course of it. He made groundless imputations against witnesses . . . insulted and trifled with the bench, and mercilessly protracted the case . . . The jury appended to their verdict a censure of the language he had employed". He was disbarred by Gray's Inn in 1874.[39] In 1968, during the speech of defence counsel to the jury, the judge said in a loud voice "Oh God", and then "laid his head across his arm and made groaning noises". The Court of Appeal dismissed the appeal on the dubious basis that the judge was only criticising the performance of the defendant's counsel and not indicating his views of the strength of the defence to the alleged crime.[40] In 1981, a judge in Tennessee told counsel during his submissions, "We shall have no more of this", and issued an injunction to restrain him from bringing any similar cases in the future.[41]

[39] *Dictionary of National Biography* (edited by Sidney Lee, 1892), volume 30, p. 411.

[40] *R* v *Hircock* [1970] 1 QB 67, 71–72.

[41] *State of Tennessee ex rel Inman* v *Brock* 622 SW 2d 36, 50 (1981) (Supreme Court of Tennessee). In June 2020, the Florida Supreme Court agreed to the emergency suspension of a lawyer accused of wasting judicial resources and making dishonest statements. The Florida Bar had

A particular favourite of mine is the oral argument by Thomas Campagne for California fruit growers in the United States Supreme Court in 1996, a performance so bad that it led to one of his clients suing him for legal malpractice even before the Supreme Court gave judgment against them. The advocate told Justice Scalia (a Justice of the Supreme Court from 1986 until his death in 2016), for some reason singling him out, "you ought to buy green plums and give them to your wife". Campagne added, to the bemusement of all, "and you're thinking to yourself right now you don't want to give your wife diarrhoea".[42]

Some of these examples are almost as bad as the advocacy of Lionel Hutz, the incompetent lawyer in the television cartoon series, *The Simpsons*:

made an application to that effect. See *The Florida Bar* v *Scot Stems* (Supreme Court of Florida, 9 June 2020) and *American Bar Association Journal*, posted 10 June 2020.

[42] The case was *Glickman* v *Wileman Brothers & Elliott Inc.* 521 US 457 (1997). See Timothy R Johnson and Jerry Goldman *A Good Quarrel: America's Top Legal Reporters Share Stories from Inside the Supreme Court* (2009), pp. 75 and 91. The legal malpractice lawsuit was settled. A great journalist, Anthony Lewis, who reported on the US Supreme Court for *The New York Times* in the 1950s and 1960s, commented, "Considering how important oral arguments can be, it is sad to say that most of them are badly done. Lawyers appearing before the Supreme Court are frequently nervous, unprepared, or, worst of all, overconfident": Anthony Lewis *The Supreme Court and How It Works* (1966), pp. 125–126, cited in Bryan A Garner *The Winning Oral Argument* (2009), p. 12.

HUTZ: I move for a bad court thing.
JUDGE: You mean a mistrial?
HUTZ: Yeah! That's why *you're* the judge and I'm a law-talking guy.
JUDGE: The lawyer.
HUTZ: Right.[43]

As others collect stamps, air miles or Impressionist paintings, I collect examples of unusual advocacy. I will refer to some of those examples in now identifying ten essential principles which I hope convey the essence of advocacy, good and bad. I echo Abraham Lincoln in his "Notes on the Practice of Law" written in around 1850 emphasising that "I find quite as much material for a lecture in those

[43] *The Simpsons*: "Marge in Chains" (1998). An infamous example of bad advocacy is the opening address to the jury by prosecuting counsel Mervyn Griffith-Jones in an obscenity trial in 1961 – "Is it a book that you would even wish your wife or your servants to read?": *The Trial of Lady Chatterley: Regina* v *Penguin Books Limited – The Transcript of the Trial* (edited by C H Rolph, 1961), p. 17. See also the advocacy of the American lawyer, Brent J Savage, in the state Supreme Court in Georgia, as described by the *American Bar Association Journal*, posted on 25 August 2021. He struggled with the questions put to him by the court, responding to an inquiry by one Justice as to whether in his answer he was hazarding a guess, "Yeah, I'm saying as a guess". He promised the court that in future he would hire someone else to "argue appellate stuff". The Oklahoma Supreme Court disbarred a lawyer, Jay Silvernail, for continuing to practise law from jail after he was convicted and sentenced for shooting and injuring a man outside an Oklahoma City nightclub. Justice Kuehn, for the court, noted that "[t]he obstacles to effective representation from a jail cell should be obvious": *State of Oklahoma ex rel Oklahoma Bar Association* v *Silvernail* (Oklahoma Supreme Court, 28 June 2022), paragraph 18.

points wherein I have failed, as in those wherein I have been moderately successful".[44]

Principle 1: Be Prepared

My first principle is that advocacy is demanding, so you must be prepared. If you wish to enjoy the confidence of the court, make sure you are in command of all the relevant facts and law. As Cicero advised, an advocate cannot "be eloquent upon a subject that is unknown to him".[45] When counsel Roger Phipps was asked in 2008 by the United States Court of Appeals for the Fifth Circuit in New Orleans why he had

[44] Abraham Lincoln "Notes on the Practice of the Law" (c. 1850) in *Abraham Lincoln: Speeches and Writings 1832–1858* (selected by Don E Fehrenbacher, 1989), p. 245.

[45] Cicero *On the Orator* (translated by E W Sutton and H Rackham, 1948), Book 1, chapter 14, p. 47. Cicero quoted the advocate Marcus Antonius as stating that "no man can speak, without the direst disgrace, on a subject which he has not mastered" (Book 2, chapter 24, p. 273). In the early nineteenth century, Serjeant Vaughan was arguing a property case despite knowing nothing of the relevant law. He told Chief Justice Gibbs, correctly (no doubt on advice from his junior), that an estate in fee simple "is the highest estate known to the law in England". The judge, making mischief, asked if he meant that. Vaughan replied that "he only meant to say it is one of the highest estates, under certain circumstances": John Lord Campbell *Lives of the Chief Justices* (1874), volume 4, pp. 297–298n. See also *R* v *K* [2008] QB 827, paragraph 8 (Lord Phillips LCJ for the Court of Appeal): "We explored with [counsel for the Crown] what the Crown's case was . . . Regrettably it seemed to us that he was considering these questions for the first time, so that he was not in a position to give us a considered response."

not addressed a relevant judgment of the Supreme Court, he replied, "I try not to read that many cases, your Honor".[46] You also need to be better prepared than the advocate reprimanded in 2011 by Judge Charles Simpson, sitting in Louisville, Kentucky, for his failure to appreciate that "Wikipedia is not an acceptable source of legal authority in the United States District Court".[47] In 2020, the United States Court of Appeals for the Eleventh Circuit criticised lawyer Peter Wizenberg for a written brief which "fails to coherently cite case law, though he cites Bugs Bunny". Counsel had summarised the opposing case and then commented, "That's all, folks!"[48] An advocate wants to avoid the experience of counsel appearing for the prosecution at Harrow Crown Court in 2005. He was asked by Judge Sanders how long he had been a barrister. When counsel replied "long

[46] *Hartz* v *Administrators of the Tulane Educational Fund* (16 April 2008, Judgment at p. 14, fn 4). After his appointment as Viceroy of India in 1921, Lord Reading, who as Rufus Isaacs had been a very successful QC before becoming Lord Chief Justice, said "I will never look at a law report again if I can help it": H Montgomery Hyde *Lord Reading* (1967), p. 327. A P Herbert's fictional Mr Justice Wool discloses in *R* v *Haddock* that "I never read the Law Reports": *Uncommon Law* (1977), p. 415. It would be unwise for counsel to submit – though understandable for a senior judge to point out – that "it is not everything that appears in the law reports that is law": *White* v *The Queen* (1962) 107 CLR 174, 175 (Dixon CJ for the High Court of Australia).

[47] *US* v *Sypher* (US District Court, Louisville, Kentucky, 9 February 2011). See *American Bar Association Journal*, posted 7 April 2011.

[48] *Wizenberg* v *Wizenberg* (US Court of Appeals for the Eleventh Circuit, 15 December 2020, No. 20-10641, p. 19). See *American Bar Association Journal*, posted 17 December 2020.

enough", the judge responded, "but everything you say is utter rubbish".[49]

Robert H. Jackson, a Justice of the US Supreme Court 1941–1954, advised advocates appearing in that court that on the day of oral argument they should "hear nothing but your case, see nothing but your case, talk nothing but your case".[50] He would have been impressed by Donald B. Verrilli Jr, Solicitor General of the United States 2011–2016, of whom a colleague said that Verrilli believed that "in the 24 hours before an [oral] argument, you should only eat salmon because it's brain food. He does that. He holes himself up with a whole mess of smoked salmon and doesn't talk to anyone".[51] Justice Jackson would not have been impressed by the lawyer arguing a case in a federal court in the United States in the 1970s who told the judge that his closing submissions would not take long because "I would like to move my car before 5 o'clock".[52]

49 *The Daily Telegraph* 17 September 2005. See also *R* v *Young and Robinson* (1978) *Criminal Law Review* 163, 164: the Court of Appeal (Criminal Division) allowed an appeal against conviction because the defendant "had been led into a trap by his own counsel". The trial judge should have intervened: "It had long been a principle that judges should protect the accused. It was rare that they had to protect them from their own counsel."

50 Clare Cushman *Courtwatchers: Eyewitness Accounts in Supreme Court History* (2011), p. 138.

51 *National Law Journal*, 31 January 2011. In fiction see Scott Turow *Innocent* (2010), p. 370: "To try a case, you ignored everything in the universe – family occasions, the news, other cases."

52 *US* v *Benn* 476 F 2d 1127, 1134 n29 (1973) (US Court of Appeals). In June 2021, Chad Hatfield realised five minutes into his oral argument before the United States Court of Appeals, Ninth Circuit, in San Francisco that he was arguing the wrong case. The court had listed a case

Justice Jackson's advice was too extreme. Counsel need to live their lives as well as argue cases. They should not take as their model Serjeant Hill, the eighteenth-century advocate of whom it was said that on his wedding night he went to his chambers in the Temple and remained there reading cases "till next morning . . . and forgot his bride".[53]

For some advocates, concentrating on one case is impossible. According to his obituary in *The Times*, Gavin

of his different to the one he expected to be arguing. The judges gave him ten minutes to find his documents for the right case before continuing: *American Bar Association Journal*, posted 14 June 2021. "'I forgot' is not an acceptable excuse" for counsel who fails to attend a hearing: *Cotto* v *City of New York* (US Court of Appeals for the Second Circuit, 19 May 2020). But the Florida District Court of Appeal, Fourth District, held in 2016 that a judge should not have barred a lawyer from arguing a case after he arrived early at court, saw that the other side's lawyer was not present, went off for a bathroom break, and returned to find the judge and the other lawyer wrapping up the hearing: *Natiello* v *Winn Dixie-Stores Inc* (Florida District Court of Appeal, Fourth District, 16 November 2016) and *American Bar Association Journal*, posted 22 November 2016.

[53] John Lord Campbell *Lives of the Lord Chancellors* (5th edition, 1868), volume 9, p. 142. The singer Michael Jackson said in 2004 that he had sacked the two lead lawyers defending him on charges of child molestation because he needed "the full attention of those who are representing me". However, "people familiar with Mr Jackson's defence" said that the lawyers had been sacked for expressing disapproval of "Mr Jackson moonwalking atop an SUV to the cheers of his fans after leaving the courthouse" on the day of his first court appearance: *New York Times* 27 April 2004. Michael Jackson was found not guilty by the jury: *New York Times* 13 June 2005. He sent each of the jurors an armband inscribed "Love always": *The Times* 21 July 2005. On Michael Jackson and his lawyers see also Chapter 2 at n. 6.

Lightman QC (later a High Court judge) "once attended 14 court hearings and conferences in a single day".[54] Even if you have one case a day, focusing on it may require exceptional efforts to avoid distractions. Marcia Clark had a very difficult time as lead prosecution counsel in the trial of O. J. Simpson for murdering his ex-wife and her friend. Ms Clark faced ruthless opponents, an incompetent judge, and a worldwide television audience of hundreds of millions of people critical of her strategy, her appearance and her child-care arrangements. Life at the bar brings many unusual experiences. But Marcia Clark is, I think, unique in appearing in court on the morning after a tabloid magazine published topless photographs of her sold to it by her ex-mother-in-law. All advocates have difficult cases, but not many of us can say, as did Marcia Clark in her memoirs, that "a Holocaust survivor sent me a book on coping".[55]

Some events at trial are unpredictable in their detail, but foreseeable in principle. As Quintilian noted, "[w]hat causes advocates most stress is the evidence".[56] Or something wholly unforeseeable may occur in court. In 2017, Miami

[54] *The Times* 4 August 2020.

[55] Marcia Clark (with Teresa Carpenter) *Without a Doubt* (1997), pp. 293–295 and p. 327. See also at pp. 327–328: "I think what touched me most was a letter sent by a convent of Dominican nuns" which "urged courage and fortitude . . . I taped it to the wall next to my desk and turned to it several times a day for comfort." Marcia Clark's cross-examination and submissions were unsuccessful, but the US$4.2 million book deal provided some solace.

[56] Quintilian *The Orator's Education*, Book 5, chapter 7 (edited and translated by Donald A Russell, 2001), p. 337.

defence attorney, Stephen Gutierrez, set fire to his trousers while making his closing speech to the jury.[57] A great advocate of the late twentieth century, James Comyn QC, wrote that the most embarrassing moment during his distinguished career was when his braces gave way and his trousers began to fall down while he was addressing the Court of Appeal.[58]

[57] *Miami Herald* 8 March 2017. Mr Gutierrez blamed a faulty battery in an e-cigarette in his pocket. He was arguing the defence of a client accused of arson. The client's defence case, like his advocate's trousers, was toast. Arguing a case in Montana, USA, an advocate set fire to his own trousers by nervously playing with some matches in his pocket: Ron Liebman *Shark Tales* (2000), p. 131.

[58] James Comyn *Summing It Up* (1991), p. 177. Counsel may need to seek an adjournment if part of the trial evidence has been eaten by his dog, as barrister Stephen Rich explained to the Newcastle Crown Court in 2000: *Daily Telegraph* 21 January 2000. Barrister Tanoo Mylvaganam's papers were blown onto the railway track at York Station by a strong gust of wind as she arrived to argue a Crown Court case. Trains were halted while staff and other passengers retrieved the documents: *Daily Telegraph* 26 February 1997. Both prosecuting and defence counsel were taken ill after eating a curry at lunchtime in the canteen at Guildford Crown Court in 1997: *Daily Telegraph* 26 November 1997. In disciplinary proceedings against barrister Henry Hendron, decided on 20 May 2021, the Bar Tribunal (Chairman, His Honour James Meston QC) dismissed a charge that Mr Hendron had appeared in a case before a Master in the Queen's Bench Division when he did not hold a practising certificate. The tribunal noted Mr Hendron's evidence that another lawyer was due to argue the case "but on the morning of the hearing [Mr Hendron's] dog had excreted over [the other lawyer's] trousers" and the other lawyer was "in a fuzzy place . . . in a daze". The other lawyer disputed this account. The tribunal did not need to decide whose account was correct. Mr Hendron was reprimanded for other disciplinary offences. See also the – rather more excitable – report of the hearing in *Mail Online*, 18 March 2021, under the headline "Disgraced

In Falkirk Sheriff Court in 1994, a lawyer struggled for ten minutes to turn off his musical socks, a Christmas present.[59]

Some hazards can be avoided by taking sensible precautions. Michael Connolly's fictional lawyer, Mickey Haller, had some good advice for counsel about to stand up and address the jury: "I put my hand down below the table to check my zipper. You have to stand before a jury only once with your fly open and it will never happen again."[60]

However, there is no excuse for not having the relevant facts and the relevant law at your fingertips. In the 1980s, a flustered advocate appearing in the United States Supreme Court was searching in vain through the documents for the answer to a question from Justice Scalia. The silence was interrupted by Justice Scalia suggesting: "just shout bingo when you find it".[61] And bear in mind the embarrassment of defence counsel in a criminal trial reprimanded by the judge in 1985 for the lack of preparation before his closing speech: "you required prompting from the prosecution and the court – and even from the foreman of the jury".[62] In the 1997 Australian film *The Castle*, the hopeless advocate, Dennis Denuto, is asked by the judge what section of the Australian Constitution he says has been breached. There is a painfully long pause as Denuto shuffles his papers.

drug-dealing barrister who bought £1,000 worth of meow meow from BBC producer blames dog that fouled on another lawyer's trousers for forcing him to risk his career".

59 *The Daily Telegraph* 18 October 1994.

60 Michael Connolly *The Fifth Witness* (2010), p. 230.

61 Henry J Abraham *Justices, Presidents and Senators* (1999), pp. 268–269.

62 *The Times* 11 April 1985.

He eventually responds, "it's just the vibe of the thing". So principle No. 1 is: be prepared.

Principle 2: Delivery

My second principle of advocacy is what Demosthenes said was the most important element of oratory: delivery. He added that it was also the second and third most important elements.[63] Aristotle advised that "it is not sufficient to have a grasp of what one should say, but one must also say these things in the way that one should".[64]

You need to speak sufficiently loudly that the judge can hear you, but without deafening them. During the trial of Michael Jackson in California in 2005 on charges of molesting a thirteen-year-old boy, the prosecutor, Tom "Mad Dog" Sneddon, "began his opening statement by shouting so loudly that the court's sound system malfunctioned".[65]

You need to speak sufficiently slowly that the judge can follow what you are saying. In a case in 2021, His Honour Judge Pelling QC complained that because insufficient time had been allocated in the time estimate for the hearing, "on the last day submissions were spoken at a speed that made

[63] Cicero *On the Orator* (translated by H Rackham, 1942), Book 3, chapter 56, p. 169. See also Quintilian *The Orator's Education*, Book 11, chapter 3 (edited and translated by Donald A Russell, 2001), pp. 87–89.

[64] Aristotle *The Art of Rhetoric* (translated by H C Lawson-Tancred, 2004), Section 9, chapter 3.1, p. 216. Aristotle added at Section 9, chapter 3.1, p. 218 that if a speech "does not indicate clearly it will not be performing its function".

[65] *The Times* 1 March 2005. On Michael Jackson see also n. 53.

them almost incomprehensible, and which led to no less than two complaints from the transcriber ... On the last of these occasions, the transcriber said she was unable to continue".[66]

You need to speak sufficiently clearly that the judge can make a note, if so inclined.[67] Appearing before some judges – Lord Hoffmann and Lord Sumption stand out in my experience – I always considered it a triumph if they made any notes at all, the rarity of that event being because, I assumed, there was little, if anything, of value that counsel could say which they had not already identified.

As Quintilian advised in the first century AD, "it is natural for judges to be more willing to believe those whom they find it easier to listen to".[68] It is surprising how many advocates cannot be understood because they are speaking too softly or too fast or indistinctly. A great American advocate of the mid-twentieth century, John W. Davis, commented that "there is no surer way to irritate the mind of any listener than to speak in so low a voice or with such indistinct articulation or in so monotonous a tone as to make the mere effort of hearing an unnecessary burden".[69] Sir

66 *Libyan Investment Authority* v *Credit Suisse International and Others* [2021] EWHC 2684 (Comm), paragraph 139,

67 Bertie Wooster tells Aunt Dahlia what had occurred and comments that "I suppose one of the top notch barristers could have put it more clearly, but not much more": P G Wodehouse *Aunts Aren't Gentlemen* (1974), chapter 13.

68 *The Orator's Education*, Book 4, chapter 1 (edited and translated by Donald A Russell, 2001), p. 185.

69 John W Davis "The Argument of an Appeal", 26 *American Bar Association Journal* 895, 896 (1940).

Terence Etherton referred at the valedictory on his retirement as Master of the Rolls in 2020 to his first case as a judge where "the advocate appearing before me spoke in a most extraordinary, unexciting way: in a kind of monotone which I'd never come across before". Sir Terence was so worried about falling asleep that he sought advice from his fellow Benchers, who told him to use smelling salts, a deep inhalation of which "made my whole body – and my head in particular – jerk back in a kind of drug-induced reaction".[70]

You cannot persuade a judge if she does not understand what you are talking about. Lord Justice Scrutton said in his judgment in a Court of Appeal case in 1929 that "there was also a third point which Norman Birkett said was difficult to express in words but which, as he never made me understand what it was, I cannot deal with".[71] I recall addressing the European Court of Human Rights in a case in the 1990s and making a light-hearted reference, for reasons which no doubt seemed sensible at the time, to the ice dance champions Torvill and Dean. It was obvious from the faces of the judges, some of whom were relying on the interpreters through headphones, that they did not have the faintest idea to whom or what I was referring. For all they knew, Torvill and Dean was a leading authority in domestic case-law which had not been mentioned in the written argument.[72]

[70] Court of Appeal Valedictory, 17 December 2020.

[71] *Tolley* v *J S Fry and Sons Ltd* [1930] 1 KB 467, 473 (Court of Appeal).

[72] See also n. 101 below on making jokes to judges in proceedings involving a translation provided by an interpreter.

Delivery does not just depend on the voice. According to Quintilian, all parts of the body are important. He attached particular significance to the eyebrows. The advocate must be careful to ensure that her eyebrows do not contradict what she is saying, or indeed contradict each other. Nostrils, Quintilian added, can be used to display “derision, contempt and disgust”.[73] In a bizarre exchange in a libel case in 1851, reference was made by Lord Chief Justice Campbell to earlier litigation where a judge had given evidence “to say how far he was influenced by a nod from counsel”.[74]

Principle 3: Focus on Your Best Points

The third principle of advocacy is to avoid the temptation to add a string of weak points to the good, or at least better, points which you can make on behalf of your client.[75] This is an old

73 Quintilian *The Orator's Education*, Book 11, chapter 1 (edited and translated by Donald A Russell, 2001), pp. 125–127. Quintilian suggested that eyebrows “signal anger if they are contracted, sadness if they are lowered, and happiness if they are relaxed. They are also moved up and down to express agreement or disagreement”. Quintilian also commended “a brief pause for reflection” as a useful tool of the advocate – “stroking the head, looking at the hand, cracking the fingers, pretending to summon up our energies, confessing nervousness by a sigh” might all come in useful: Book 11, chapter 3, p. 167.

74 *Florence* v *Lawson* 17 *Law Times* 260 (1851).

75 In *Jones* v *Barnes* 463 US 745, 751–752 (1983), Chief Justice Burger for the Supreme Court of the United States similarly stated that “[e]xperienced advocates since time beyond memory have emphasised the importance of winnowing out weaker arguments on appeal and focusing on one central issue if possible, or at most on a few key issues”. In *Ashmore* v *Corporation of Lloyds* [1992] 1 WLR 446, 453, Lord

problem. In his study of the origins of the legal profession, Professor Paul Brand referred to an advocate, Serjeant Friskney, being criticised by Chief Justice Hengham in 1305 for persisting in a line of argument which the court did not find convincing.[76] I have heard as many cases lost by the good, or at least better, argument being hidden in a mass of bad arguments as I have heard cases won by good advocacy. Quintilian advised the advocate to "press points which you see are to [the judge's] liking, and retreat smartly from those which are not well received".[77] Cicero advised to like effect, that even if you have a number of strong points, "then those among them that are the least weighty . . . ought to be discarded".[78]

Templeman said (for the Appellate Committee of the House of Lords): "It is the duty of counsel to assist the judge by simplification and concentration and not to advance a multitude of ingenious arguments in the hope that out of 10 bad points the judge will be capable of fashioning a winner. . . . [T]here has been a tendency in some cases for legal advisers, pressed by their clients, to make every point conceivable and inconceivable without judgment or discrimination."

[76] Paul Brand *The Origins of the English Legal System* (1992), p. 126.

[77] *The Orator's Education*, Book 12, chapter 10 (edited and translated by Donald A Russell, 2001), pp. 311–313. See also Book 5, chapter 12 at p. 459: "we must not always burden the judge with all the arguments we have discovered, because that both bores him and damages our credibility". The lawyers representing the Kansas Secretary of State in a case in the US District Court in 2018 about voting rights included in their written pleading an argument that the plaintiffs lacked standing to sue, and followed it with a comment in capital letters – which they had omitted to edit out – "PROBABLY NOT WORTH ARGUING?": *Kansas City Star* 24 April 2018 and *American Bar Association Journal*, posted 26 April 2018.

[78] Cicero *On the Orator* (translated by H Rackham, 1942), Book 2, chapter 76, pp. 433–435.

Abraham Lincoln had a very effective approach as an advocate: when he heard his point answered by the other side, he would respond, "Well, I reckon I must be wrong". Many of his opponents did not appreciate until too late that he was conceding only what he could not sustain, and focusing on his best points.[79] On this principle of sticking to your best points I also commend the more pungent comment attributed to an unnamed judge, that if, at a dinner party, you serve a plate of delicious items but with a turd on top of one of them, none of them will be eaten.[80]

[79] Gary Wills *Lincoln at Gettysburg* (1992), pp. 95–96, citing Leonard Swett, a lawyer who had faced Lincoln in court. See similarly Quintilian *The Orator's Education*, Book 6, chapter 4 (edited and translated by Donald A Russell, 2001), p. 131: "When defeat is inevitable, the best policy is to give way: if there are more points in dispute, you will be more easily believed on these; if there is only the one, [a] modest submission usually earns a lighter sentence."

[80] See also, but with the whiff of mid-twentieth-century sexism, Sir Malcolm Hilbery *Duty and Art in Advocacy* (1959), p. 26: "Even caviare unattractively served by a slattern can be repellent." The obituary of Conrad Dehn QC recorded that when appearing before Lord Chief Justice Widgery in the 1970s, Dehn told the court he had nineteen points to make, to which Widgery replied, "Just give us your 19th point": *The Times* 10 June 2020. See also Peter Millett *As In Memory Long* (2015), p. 68, cited by Peter Lyons *Advocacy: A Practical Guide* (2019), pp. 214–215 on an exchange between Lord Justice Lawton and counsel in the Court of Appeal:

> JUDGE: "We have read your Notice of Appeal. It raises 7 points does it not?"
>
> COUNSEL: "Yes, my Lord."

Principle 4: Address the Weaknesses in Your Argument

My fourth principle of advocacy is do not ignore the weaknesses in your argument. You need to address them. John Marshall Harlan, a Justice of the US Supreme Court in the middle of the twentieth century, commented that "[t]here is rarely a case, however strong, that does not have its weak points. And I do not know any way of meeting a weak point except to face up to it".[81] Judges will lose trust in you, and your case, if you seek to avoid or evade a weakness. In 2011 Judge Richard Posner of the United States Court of Appeals in Chicago criticised advocates in a case before him for ignoring precedents unhelpful to their argument. He observed that "the ostrich is a noble animal, but not a proper model for an appellate advocate". He illustrated his judgment with a picture of an ostrich with its head in the sand, and a picture of a suited lawyer also with his head in the sand.[82]

There is, nevertheless, an important distinction between acknowledging the weaknesses in your case and making no attempt to minimise them. In 1957, *The Times*

JUDGE: "We think that point number 4 is your best point. Do you agree?"
COUNSEL: "Er . . . yes, my Lord."
JUDGE: "Well we don't think much of it."

[81] John M Harlan "What Part Does the Oral Argument Play in the Conduct of an Appeal", 41 *Cornell Law Quarterly* 6, 9 (1955).

[82] *Gonzalez-Servin* v *Ford Motor Co* (US Court of Appeals, 7th Circuit, 23 November 2011). See *American Bar Association Journal*, posted 28 November 2011.

law report noted that Mr Justice Stable, having listened to the submissions of counsel, asked, "Is one to abandon every vestige of common sense in approaching this matter?" To which counsel replied, "Yes, my Lord".[83]

Principle 5: Respond to Questions from the Court

Principle number five is that you should welcome, and respond to, questions from the court. Do not adopt the attitude of John Mortimer's creation, the barrister Horace Rumpole, who thinks to himself: "one Judge is bad enough, but the Appeal Court comes equipped with three who bother you with unnecessary and impertinent questions which are not always easy to answer".[84] Counsel is not advised to follow the example of D. N. Pritt in a case in the Appellate Committee of the House of Lords in the 1920s or 1930s, He was facing numerous questions and observations from a hostile bench. Lord Buckmaster told him that their

[83] *Thorp* v *King Brothers (Dorking) Limited The Times* 22 February 1957 cited in R E Megarry *A New Miscellany-at-Law* (edited by Bryan A Garner, 2005), p. 295, As Lord Donaldson MR said in the Court of Appeal in *Re F* [1990] 2 AC 1, 17B, "the common law is common sense under a wig". Stephen M Shapiro "Oral Argument in the Supreme Court of the United States", 33 *Catholic University Law Review* 529, 531 (1984) pointed out that "Oral argument gives the advocate the opportunity to personally motivate the Justices to rule in his or her favour by conveying the impression that fairness, common sense and the general public interest strongly support his position".

[84] John Mortimer "Rumpole and the Rights of Man" in *Rumpole and the Angel of Death* (1995), p. 188.

Lordships "would like to know how long this nonsense is going to continue". Pritt replied: "About ten days, if interruptions continue on their present scale, and a few days less if they diminish".[85]

The advocate should recognise that questions provide an opportunity to find out and address what interests or concerns the court. Questions and comments from the court are a window into the judicial mind.[86] Justice John I. Laskin of the Court of Appeal for Ontario helpfully advised advocates that busy judges "want answers to two questions: can you help us and how fast?"[87]

You cannot help the court, and persuade the judges on behalf of your client, if you resent interruptions as a distraction from presenting the argument you have prepared. Justice Scalia of the US Supreme Court told advocates in a speech in 2009 that when a judge asks them to comment on a hypothetical example, it is because he wishes to test the submission being made, and it does not assist the court for the lawyer to respond "it's not this case". As Scalia pointed out, "I know it's not this case, you idiot".[88] An experienced advocate before the United States Supreme Court, Stephen M. Shapiro, wisely advised that counsel's "prepared remarks

[85] See Alan Paterson *The Law Lords* (1982), p. 68.

[86] And "[i]f the question does nothing more it gives you assurance that the court is not comatose and that you have awakened at least a vestigial interest": John W Davis "The Argument of an Appeal", 26 *American Bar Association Journal* 895, 897 (1940).

[87] Justice John I Laskin "What Persuades (or What's Going on Inside the Judge's Mind)", 23(1) *The Advocates' Society Journal* 6 (2004).

[88] *Texas Lawyer* 29 June 2009.

should expand or contract like an accordion" in response to questioning, seeking to incorporate points you want to make into your answers.[89]

Ruth Bader Ginsburg, a Justice of the United States Supreme Court for twenty-seven years until her death in 2020, spoke of the damage to an advocate's case when he answered a question from that bench by saying, "Forgive me, Your Honour, but I really don't want to be derailed onto that trivial point".[90] If it matters to the judge, then it should matter to the advocate. Do not reply to questions from the judge as did an advocate in a District of Columbia court in 1969 by saying that I have not come to court "to listen to a whole lot of stuff from you; I am not in the mood for it".[91]

Counsel sometimes forget that the object of the exercise is to persuade, not to lecture the judge or show their client how combative they are in confronting an unreceptive judge. Some clients congratulate their advocates after the hearing because "you really told her". Wiser clients recognise that a more valuable service is performed by the advocate who has a conversation with the court because that means that she is at least part of the way towards persuading the bench. I did once have a client who was delighted that the other side had not

[89] Stephen M Shapiro *Oral Argument in the Supreme Court: The Felt Necessities of the Time* (1985 Address before the Supreme Court Historical Society) (available on the Mayer Brown website), p. 10.

[90] Ruth Bader Ginsburg, "Remarks for University of Virginia Student Legal Forum Dinner" (1990), cited in Bryan A Garner *The Winning Oral Argument* (2009), p. 173.

[91] *In the Matter of George D Gates* 248 A 2d 671 (1968) (District of Columbia Court of Appeals).

been called on during our appeal in the Judicial Committee of the Privy Council. "There you are", he told me, "the judges were not interested in what the other side had to say."[92]

Principle 6: Plain Speaking

The sixth principle of advocacy is that plain speaking is usually far more effective than florid oratory.[93] What was effective for a great advocate of the early twentieth century, Sir Edward Marshall Hall – "Look at her, Gentlemen of the jury, look at her. God never gave her a chance. Won't you? Won't you?"[94] – would today be met with embarrassment or, even worse, sniggering.[95] The guide for counsel appearing in

[92] In the nineteenth century, Alexander Cockburn (later the Lord Chief Justice) had an unsettling experience as a young barrister. He argued a motion in the court of Lord Chancellor Brougham who was "engrossed with his correspondence, and took no notice of the argument except to say curtly at the conclusion of counsel's speech, 'Motion refused'". But the story had a happy ending because, a few months later, Cockburn was delighted to receive a series of briefs from a solicitor who told Cockburn that he had been in court that day and was most impressed that the Lord Chancellor was "taking down every word you said". See J B Atlay *The Victorian Chancellors* (1908), volume 2, p. 20n.

[93] "Nothing detailed, subtle or rhetorical ever gets across during oral argument: Stephen M Shapiro "Oral Argument in the Supreme Court of the United States", 33 *Catholic University Law Review* 529, 538 (1984).

[94] Lord Birkett *Six Great Advocates* (1961), p. 16.

[95] Cicero recommended "a style that is dignified and graceful": *On the Orator* (translated by E W Sutton and H Rackham, 1948), Book 1, chapter 12, p. 41. Though this did provoke Quintilian to observe that Cicero was "a rude ignoramus": *The Orator's Education*, Book 8, Introduction (edited and translated by Donald A Russell, 2001), p. 321.

the United States Supreme Court wisely advises: "Avoid emotional oration and loud, impassioned pleas."[96] Styles change. In the early years of the United States Supreme Court, "the emotional rhetoric of counsel brought tears to the eyes of" Chief Justice Marshall on at least two occasions.[97]

As with all these principles of advocacy, there are many exceptions to the principle that counsel should avoid emotional pleas. Manhattan attorney Mo Levine was said to be so skilful that he sold tape recordings of his final arguments. In one personal injuries case, Levine represented a man who had both hands amputated in an accident. His entire closing speech to the jury was: "ladies and gentlemen, I just had lunch with my client. He ... eats ... like ... a ... dog".[98]

In 1961. Lord Birkett, in his book *Six Great Advocates*, suggested that it helps counsel if "he knows the Bible in the Authorized Version, and if he has made the

[96] *Guide for Counsel in Cases to Be Argued before the Supreme Court* (2012), p. 11.

[97] R. Strickland "The Court and the Trail of Tears", *Supreme Court Historical Society Yearbook* 20, 26 (1979), cited by Stephen M Shapiro "Oral Argument in the Supreme Court: The Felt Necessities of the Time" (1985 Address before the Supreme Court Historical Society) (available on the Mayer Brown website), p. 2.

[98] Roy Grutman and Bill Thomas *Lawyers and Thieves* (1990), p. 56. A (very successful) New York jury advocate, Izzy Halpern, noted for his emotional style, was interrupted in full flow by a woman on a jury in Brooklyn: "It's not worth it. You're going to have a heart attack" – David Margolick *At the Bar* (1995), p. 162. See also Chapter 2 at nn. 138–140 on appeals being allowed because of inappropriate emotional rhetoric by counsel.

language of the book of Common Prayer his very own".[99] Not today in the St Albans Crown Court or in the Supreme Court.

Principle 7: Avoid Humour (unless You Are a Stand-Up Comedian)

My seventh principle of advocacy is that humour is a very unreliable weapon in court – however valuable it may be in helping to maintain the attention of those attending a lecture or reading a book – to be avoided in other than exceptional circumstances. Aristotle referred to "destroy[ing] the seriousness of the other [speaker] with laughter and their laughter with seriousness".[100] But there are very few advocates who can laugh the opposing case out of court. One of them was Abraham Lincoln. When acting for a defendant in a civil case, Lincoln stood to address the jury, slowly picked up the plaintiff's petition, scrutinized it closely and "indulged in a long loud laugh accompanied by his most wonderfully grotesque facial expression". The judge, jury and public gallery joined in the laughter. The jury made a small award of damages to the plaintiff.[101]

99 Lord Birkett *Six Great Advocates* (1961), p. 109.

100 Aristotle *The Art of Rhetoric* (translated by H C Lawson-Tancred, 2004), Section 10, chapter 3.18, p. 260.

101 Albert A Woldman *Lawyer Lincoln* (1994), p. 128. Michael Beloff QC stated in *Advocacy as Art: Margaret Howard Memorial Lecture 2000* (Oxford, 18 May 2000) that "No sterner test of the advocate is presented than trying, in Strasbourg, to make – in translation – a smile flit across the flintlike face of the Icelandic judge" – Michael Beloff QC was one of the very few advocates I have heard with the ability to

The guide for counsel published by the United States Supreme Court wisely advises that "[a]ttempts at humour usually fall flat".[102] So it is better to take the opposing case seriously.[103] Most judges prefer to decide for themselves when to make jokes – and if they do, advocates are advised to laugh however unfunny they may be.[104] For an advocate to attempt

produce such an effect. Note also Lord Rodger "Humour and Law", 33 *SLT* (News) 202, 211 (2009): "With international tribunals a lack of humour is indeed almost inevitable since successful humour depends, to a large extent, on shared cultural assumptions which tend to have a national or, at least, linguistic base. Hence there are no (intentional) jokes in judgments of the European Court of Justice or the European Court of Human Rights." See n. 72 above for my unsuccessful attempt at a light-hearted reference in the latter court.

102 *Guide for Counsel in Cases to Be Argued before the Supreme Court* (2012), p. 11. See also Lord Rodger "Humour and Law", 33 *SLT* (News) 202, 205 (2009): "on the whole, counsel do best to leave the jokes to the judges".

103 Quintilian *The Orator's Education*, Book 1, chapter 11, p. 237: the orator "will keep well clear of staginess and of anything excessive in facial expression". Quintilian adds, at Book 6, chapter 3, p. 79, advice to advocates to avoid "the rough humour of the buffoon or the stage". He suggests advocates should only make jokes if the context of the case permits: "No one will tolerate a prosecutor who makes jokes in a horrendous case, or a defence advocate who does so in one that commands pity."

104 In Lord Eldon's court in the early nineteenth century, "[w]henever it was indicated, by a peculiar elevation of his eyebrow, that he meant to be jocular, it is said that the gentlemen of the Chancery Bar were thrown into an ecstasy of mirth": John Lord Campbell *Lives of the Lord Chancellors* (5th edition, 1868), volume 10, p. 290. Mr Justice Darling (appointed to the Bench in 1897) "would lie back in his chair staring at the ceiling with the back of his head cupped in his hands paying scant attention to any argument but waiting until some footling little joke

a joke runs a very large risk of misjudging the mood of the court. Mr Jay Floyd, counsel for the State of Texas, began his argument before the United States Supreme Court in 1971 in the abortion rights case of *Roe* v *Wade* by referring to the two female counsel for the plaintiff: "It's an old joke, but when a man argues against two beautiful ladies like this, they're going to have the last word." No-one laughed.[105]

Professor Arthur Goodhart went too far in suggesting that "a sense of humour is not an essential part of the successful barrister's equipment".[106] A sense of humour, and indeed a sense of the ridiculous, assist counsel to deal with the trials and tribulations of practice as an advocate. Conrad Dehn QC recalled that, as a very junior barrister in the late 1950s, he saw the judge smiling at him during his submissions at Croydon County Court. Counsel returned the smile. "What

occurred to his mind. When this happened he would make the joke, the court would echo for about thirty seconds with sycophantic laughter, and then the process would start over again": C P Harvey QC *The Advocate's Devil* (1958), p. 33. Harvey added at p. 52 that "it is unpleasing to laymen to witness the extravagances of bootlicking to which counsel must sometimes condescend in order to preserve the goodwill of the tribunal". In fiction, see Ian McEwan *The Children Act* (2014), p. 60: the judge's occasional weak joke in court is "fawningly received by counsel for both sides". And Scott Turow *Innocent* (2010), p. 109: "As I discovered long ago, being a judge somehow makes your every joke, even the lamest, side splitting".

105 *May It Please the Court: The Most Significant Oral Arguments Made before the Supreme Court since 1955* (edited by Peter Irons and Stephanie Guitton), pp. 146–147 and Antonin Scalia and Bryan A Garner *Making Your Case: The Art of Persuading Judges* (2008), p. 186.

106 Professor Arthur L Goodhart *Five Jewish Lawyers of the Common Law* (1949), p. 49.

are you smiling at?", demanded the judge angrily. "I thought Your Honour was smiling at me, so I smiled back", the barrister replied. "I was not smiling", said the judge. "I was grimacing at the pain of my war wound."[107]

My point, my seventh principle, is that it is rarely helpful for the advocate to make jokes in court.

Principle 8: But Do Not Bore the Court

Principle number eight is that although the court will be receptive to plain speaking, and jokes normally fall flat in court, the advocate must avoid boring the judge or jury. You want them to focus on your submissions, and the best way to do that is to make what you say interesting. As noted by Jonathan Sumption (a very distinguished advocate before his appointment to the Supreme Court in 2012), "you should never underestimate the importance of entertainment as a tool of advocacy".[108]

John Mortimer QC suggested a contrary principle: that "[b]oredom is a weapon you can use in court; given sufficient endurance you can bore a judge into submission by going on until he's in real danger of missing his train to Hayward's Heath and is ready to submit".[109] The modern

[107] Conrad Dehn QC *Graya News* (Summer 2006).

[108] Jonathan Sumption *Law in a Time of Crisis* (2021), p. 7. See also Stephen M Shapiro "Oral Argument in the Supreme Court of the United States", 33 *Catholic University Law Review* 529, 539 (1984): "[T]he advocate should remember that the greatest barrier to an effective argument is boredom."

[109] John Mortimer *Murderers and Other Friends* (1994), p. 58.

requirement that judges maintain efficient case management makes such a tactic very unlikely to succeed today, if it ever did.

Counsel have sometimes – and occasionally successfully – made allusions to history or fiction in the hope that such interesting references may distract attention away from the weaknesses in their case.[110] In 1932, in allowing an appeal from a judgment on a claim by a husband that another man had enticed away his wife, Lord Justice Scrutton in the Court of Appeal criticised the trial judge for allowing "some ingenious counsel" to divert his attention by suggesting that "there was some likeness between this case and the Trojan War".[111] The lawyers acting for Joaquin Guzman ("El Chapo"), on trial in Brooklyn, New York, and later convicted, for running the world's largest drug cartel, creatively compared their client to Jean Valjean, the persecuted hero of *Les Miserables*.[112]

Counsel may decide to use vivid imagery to describe her client or the opposing case. Vincent Fuller, counsel for the

[110] But see Chapter 2 at n. 140 for a court allowing an appeal because of what it considered to be an inappropriate literary allusion.

[111] *Place* v *Searle* 48 TLR 428, 429 (1932).

[112] *The Times* 5 November 2018. Other allusions to popular culture include the submissions of Michael Hubbard QC on behalf of Maxine Carr, accused of assisting her boyfriend, Ian Huntley, to murder two girls. Counsel told the jury: "if she was allowed to say anything to you now she may echo the lines of that classic song [by Englebert Humperdinck], 'Please release me, let me go. For I don't love him any more'". The jury convicted her of conspiracy to pervert the course of justice and she was sentenced to three and a half years' imprisonment: *The Times* 12 December 2003.

boxer, Mike Tyson, on trial for (and convicted of) rape, poetically, and creatively, described his client as "A sensitive, thoughtful, caring man. A tulip among weeds".[113] Howard Fensterman, the attorney for a nursing home in Long Island, New York, responding to a complaint by the family of a resident that an adult entertainment show had been organised there, said: "This lawsuit has the worth of toilet paper that is about to be flushed".[114]

Counsel may even insult or denigrate his own client in order to attract the attention of the jury and obtain the best possible result – though it is wise to alert the client in advance. The television presenter and actress Donna Air was cleared of parking permit fraud by a jury at Isleworth Crown Court in 2012 after her counsel, Benn Maguire, told the jury that his client had not read the terms and conditions of the permit because "I suspect there's not a great deal going on in Ms Air's head . . . other than hot air".[115] An appeal was unsuccessfully brought in 1991 against the conviction of Baron Michael De Stempel, jailed for four years for helping his ex-wife to steal from her wealthy aunt. The unsuccessful grounds of appeal included that trial counsel, Richard Du Cann QC, in his closing speech to the jury, had described his client, the defendant, as "a congenital liar" and "a monumental snob". Rejecting the application for permission to appeal, the Court of Appeal said that Mr Du Cann's tactics has been "understandable and convincing" – he was seeking to persuade the jury that lying was a normal part of the defendant's behaviour

[113] *The Observer* 29 March 1992. [114] *The Times* 10 April 2014.
[115] *The Times* 30 March 2012.

and so did not necessarily link him to a dishonest plan.[116] In the 1933 Marx Brothers film *Duck Soup*, Groucho as Rufus T. Firefly addresses the Bench on behalf of Chico: "Gentlemen, Chicolini here may talk like an idiot and look like an idiot, but don't let that fool you. He really is an idiot."[117]

Counsel have employed a wide variety of styles in order to capture the attention of judge or jury. Lord Birkett described how Sir Edward Marshall Hall KC for the defence in a murder case early in the twentieth century acted out for the jury "the moment when the pistol went off and the husband fell". Marshall Hall let the pistol drop to the floor of the courtroom and "the sudden breaking of the intense stillness of the court by the noise of the falling pistol produced the most extraordinary effect on everybody present, almost as though they had witnessed the actual tragedy itself".[118]

A modern imitator, less successful, of this theatrical style was Bruce Cutler, the lawyer for John Gotti and others accused of organised crime in New York in the 1990s. He

[116] *The Independent* 8 November 1991. Barrister Jeremy Wickham was, in 2016, defending a man, Juan Calero, who sneaked into the home of a family friend, riffled through her underwear and committed a sex act on her bed, conduct recorded by a hidden camera installed by his victim. Mr Wickham sensibly submitted to the court in mitigation that it would take "an instant dislike to my client" for his "truly despicable act" for which "there is no excuse". Calero was given an eighteen-week jail sentence, suspended for two years: *The Times* 23 August 2016.

[117] See Fred R Shapiro *Oxford Dictionary of American Legal Quotations* (1993), p. 376.

[118] Lord Birkett *Six Great Advocates* (1961), pp. 15–16.

liked ostentatiously to slam the indictment into a wastepaper basket in front of the jury.[119] One of his colleagues in defending mob cases, Gerald Shargel, would make part of his closing speech from the witness box: "You remember, he sat right *here*!"[120] In a case in New York in 1944, defence counsel "picked up a candlestick and struck himself on the head with it to show its ineffectiveness as a murder weapon". His client was convicted, and counsel was left with a headache.[121] In 2002, a California defence attorney, Nedra Ruiz, known for her dramatic style of advocacy, represented a husband and wife accused (and convicted) of owning two dogs that attacked and killed a neighbour in San Francisco. During the jury trial, Ruiz "crawled across the courtroom floor" to depict the fatal struggle. She "kicked the jury box . . . cried and screamed".[122]

So my eighth principle is try to keep your submissions interesting, though in some of these examples, counsel may have forgotten the wise words of Lord Esher MR in a

[119] Frederic Dannen "Defending the Mafia" *The New Yorker* 21 February 1994, p. 64 at p. 80. Cutler was so aggressive in cross-examination that witnesses were said to have been "Brucified".

[120] Frederic Dannen "Defending the Mafia" *The New Yorker* 21 February 1994, p. 64 at p. 67.

[121] Dominick Dunne *Justice* (2001), p. 288.

[122] *Court tv.com* 8 March 2002 and *CNN.com* 26 March 2002. In 2004, Jeffrey Kaufman, a Florida defence attorney, representing a Disney World worker acquitted of fondling a child while posing in costume for a photograph with her and her mother, gave part of his closing argument dressed in a Tigger outfit "to show jurors how difficult it is to manoeuvre and see in the outfit": *CNN.com* 4 August 2004.

case in 1889: counsel is not "bound to degrade himself for the purpose of winning his client's case".[123]

Principle 9: Do Not Lose Your Temper with the Judge or Your Opponents or Insult Them (however Strong the Provocation)

A ninth principle: however strong the provocation, and sometimes it will be considerable, an advocate must not lose her temper or seek to insult her opponent or the judge. You will simply demean yourself.

As stated in the guide for counsel appearing in the United States Supreme Court, "[d]o not denigrate opposing counsel. It is appropriate and effective to be courteous to your opponent".[124] Chief Judge Lee H. Rosenthal began a judgment in the US District Court in Houston, Texas in 2020 by stating: "One of the sentences a judge does not imagine – much less welcome – writing includes the words 'butt shaking' in describing a lawyer's alleged actions at a mediation. Sadly those words fit here." The judge decided that no sanction was required because the lawyer concerned had withdrawn from the case and the national press reports of the proceedings had damaged his professional reputation, and therefore his ability to attract new business, "and they should".[125]

[123] *In Re G Mayor Cooke* (1889) 5 TLR 407, 408 (Court of Appeal).

[124] *Guide for Counsel in Cases to Be Argued before the Supreme Court* (2012), p. 11.

[125] *White* v *Chevron Phillips Chemical Co* (US District Court for the Southern District of Texas, Houston Division, 4 May 2020). In *Wiegand* v *Royal Caribbean Cruises Ltd* (20 April 2021) Judge Donald L Graham

It would be wise to avoid following the example of Adam "Bulletproof" Reposa (as he described himself on the website of the Texas State Bar) who was sentenced to ninety days in jail for his conduct as defence counsel at a hearing in 2009. He was found in contempt of court for making, during the proceedings, a "simulated masturbatory gesture" as an insulting response to the submissions made by the prosecutor. Justice Womack for the Texas Court of Criminal Appeals rejected the ambitious argument presented on behalf of Mr Reposa at the contempt hearing that he was simply "performing his duty of zealously representing his client or advancing his client's case".[126] In 2021, a Chicago lawyer, Edwin Franklin Bush III of Des Plaines, Illinois, admitted to the Illinois Attorney Registration and Disciplinary Commission that he had called an opposing lawyer a "lowlife bottom-feeder" but he contended that his comments were "truthful or constitutionally protected speech".[127]

However much you may resent the submissions made by your opponent, do not respond in the manner of counsel in the US state of Indiana in 1978, who was disbarred

of the United States District Court in Miami, Florida criticised counsel in a civil claim for the lack of civility in the written pleadings from both sides which were "riddled with inflammatory language and insults directed at the parties and their counsel" such that they read like "a script from a tabloid *Jerry Springer* television show". He ordered that the pleadings be struck out, and that they be refiled using only appropriate language: *American Bar Association Journal*, posted 4 May 2021.

[126] *Ex parte Adam Reposa* (Court of Criminal Appeals of Texas, 28 October 2009); and see *Texas Lawyer* 29 October 2009.

[127] *American Bar Association Journal*, posted 8 September 2021.

for violations of disciplinary rules, including telling a court that his opponent was "so lacking in mental capacity as not being able to find his way to the toilet".[128] Do not answer a submission by your opponent that you are "a big mouth" by grabbing your opponent by the throat to try to choke him, as occurred in the judge's chambers in New Jersey in 1976; the Supreme Court of New Jersey severely reprimanded the attorney for conduct which resulted in "the judge, his law clerk and the two attorneys ... rolling on the floor. The judge suffered minor injuries before the two combatants could be separated".[129] Do not ask the jury, in your closing submissions for the defence, "if they would play miniature golf with the prosecutor" or "buy a used car from the prosecutor".[130] Do not tell opposing counsel during a deposition (that is a formal questioning of a witness before trial) that they were "not dicking around with a rookie" and "can I like fly up to North Dakota and just fucking hit you right in the middle of the forehead, with an upper cut?"[131]

[128] *In the Matter of Owen W Crumpacker* 383 NE 2d 36, 48 (1978) (Supreme Court of Indiana). The Supreme Court of the United States declined to intervene: 444 US 979 (1979).

[129] *In the Matter of Dennis D S McAlvey* 354 A 2d 289, 290 (1976).

[130] *Tarrant* v *State of Florida* 537 So 2d 150, 152 (1989), where the District Court of Appeal in Florida found counsel in contempt of court.

[131] *Avery* v *E & M Services* (US District Court for the District of North Dakota, Case No. 1:18-cv-258, 15 December 2020), where US Magistrate Judge Clare Hochhalter reprimanded counsel Todd Alan Stubbs for his conduct during the deposition. Judge Hochhalter declined to impose a financial sanction because "Stubbs has endured the indignities of being fired by plaintiff in the middle of a deposition and of having his churlishness and general lack of professionalism

Lord Chief Justice Thomas of Cwmgiedd said for the Court of Appeal in a 2015 case[132] that counsel should not, in a speech to the jury, make "personal criticism of opposing advocates in contradistinction to criticism of the prosecution case". But there are exceptional occasions when counsel considers that a personal attack on an opponent is necessary to protect the interests of the client. In 1992, in his closing speech to the jury in a libel case, Richard Hartley QC for the claimant attacked the forensic methods adopted by opposing counsel, George Carman QC. Mr Hartley complained that Mr Carman had presented during the trial "a music-hall turn as a stand-up comic". His cross-examination of the claimant had been "cruel and cowardly".[133]

Counsel should never insult the judge. Again, this is an old problem. At the end of the thirteenth century, a lawyer was suspended from practice for having complained that all

memorialized for posterity in this order. This is sanction enough". See *American Bar Association Journal*, posted 17 December 2020.

[132] *R* v *Ekaireb* [2015] EWCA Crim 1936, paragraphs 59–60.

[133] *The Times* 22 September 1992. There was no excuse for the conduct of barrister Althea Brown who, on 12 March 2022, was fined £1,500 (and ordered to pay £5,820 costs) by the Bar Standards Board Disciplinary Tribunal for her rudeness to the opposing barrister in an employment tribunal hearing. Ms Brown had mocked her opponent's submissions by repeating her words "in a noticeable different and disrespectful tone of voice to her usual voice", and had insulted her opponent by suggesting that she had a "fundamental intellectual difficulty" and by comparing her submissions to the words of the child, Violet Bott, in Richmal Crompton's *Just William* stories who said, "I'm going to scream and scream until I'm sick". See *The Times* 2 June 2002 and *Daily Mail* 2 June 2022.

the justices of the court were evil and "shrews".[134] In 2020, a fine of £1,000 was imposed on a barrister, Marguerite Russell, by a Bar disciplinary tribunal for "pulling faces at the judge" during proceedings, for stating "this is ridiculous" and describing the judge's decision as "insane" following rulings rejecting submissions she had made.[135]

There are much more colourful examples of errant counsel behaviour in the United States. It is not a good idea to tell a judge in response to a ruling, "that's a bunch of bunk and you know it . . . Let the record reflect that the judge is an unmitigated liar, unmitigated, unequivocal liar"; the Supreme Court of Ohio suspended counsel from practice for one year.[136] It is not good advocacy for counsel to shout at a judge during a telephone conference in a family law matter that he was "a narcissistic, maniacal mental case and should not be on the bench"; the Illinois Supreme Court suspended lawyer Melvin H Hoffman from practice for six months in 2010 for this and other offensive statements.[137] In 2015, Kathryn B. Abele was suspended from practice for a year

[134] Paul Brand *The Origins of the English Legal System* (1992), p. 134.

[135] *The Times* 6 June 2020. A criminal law barrister, Jacqueline Vallejo, was fined £2,000 and suspended from practice for four months by a Bar disciplinary tribunal for her persistent rudeness to a judge in a case. She was "belligerent", she created a "toxic atmosphere in court", and told the jury that the judge's summary of the evidence was "absolute rubbish". See *The Times* 17 June 2022.

[136] *Bar Association of Greater Cleveland* v *Carlin* 423 NE 2d 477, 478n and 479n (1981) (Supreme Court of Ohio).

[137] *Re Melvin H Hoffman* (Supreme Court of Illinois, 22 September 2010) and *Report and Recommendation of the Review Board of the Illinois Attorney Registration and Disciplinary Commission* (23 June 2010).

by the Supreme Court of the State of Washington for various disciplinary offences which included making in court what the judge described as "loud noises, that to me sounded like an animal being killed". She was "screaming, yelling, jumping up and down in my courtroom, stomping and then – stomping out".[138]

If you want to persuade a court to reopen a case after it has given summary judgment, it is unlikely to be helpful for counsel to file a statement telling the judges that "THIS IS LA LA LAND ON STEROIDS . . . This is so bizarro land that it is hard to type" (capitals in the original), or in a motion to reargue another case, to tell the court "Nice joke.

[138] *In the Matter of the Disciplinary Proceedings against Kathryn B Abele* (Supreme Court of the State of Washington, 27 August 2015). There are many such cases. In 1994, the Wisconsin Court of Appeals affirmed a trial court finding of contempt and a fine of $250 on a defence lawyer who exclaimed "ridiculous" when her client's sentence was announced by the judge: *Oliveto* v *Circuit Court for Crawford County* 519 NW 2d 769 (1994). Alison Motta of Chicago was suspended from practice for ninety days in 2017 for her "unprofessional disruptive" conduct during a trial. After unfavourable rulings from the judge rejecting her objections to evidence, in the presence of the jury she would "shake her head, roll her eyes and make comments under her breath". On one such occasion she commented that the ruling was "fucking bullshit". This was after multiple warnings from the judge about her behaviour: *In the matter of the Discipline of Alison Hope Motta* (US District Court for the Northern District of Illinois, 8 May 2017) and *Chicago Tribune* 12 May 2017. Judge David Borowski of Milwaukee County, Wisconsin ordered the detention (for about fifteen minutes) of defence lawyer, Puck Tsai, for contempt of court, for "rolling your eyes, throwing your hands in the air, acting like I'm some kind of idiot": *Milwaukee Journal Sentinel* 31 October 2018 and *American Bar Association Journal*, posted 30 October 2018.

DISGUSTING"; counsel, Gino L. Giorgini III, was suspended from practice for three months by the Supreme Court of New York, Appellate Division, in 2018 for comments which "went beyond the bounds of zealous advocacy and were derogatory, undignified and inexcusable" and accused the court of political bias and corruption.[139] In 2020, the Ohio Supreme Court suspended attorney Thomas Alan Yoder from practice for two years for various disciplinary offences, which included complaining that a magistrate's decision was "the most absolutely insane decision" he had ever encountered and writing to tell counsel for an opposing party that "you are a complete idiot . . . [Y]ou are too stupid to know how stupid you are".[140]

The winner of the prize for the offensive submission least likely to persuade the court is Michael J. Anderson, a North Carolina attorney, who faced disciplinary charges in 2015 for his comments in pleadings about the State Court of Appeals judges, including: "Had I known the level of intellectual functioning and maturity of this panel in advance, I would have come prepared with a colouring book with big

[139] *In the Matter of Gino L Giorgini III* (Supreme Court of New York, Appellate Division, 25 September 2018); *New York Times* 13 October 2018.

[140] *Toledo Bar Association* v *Yoder* (6 October 2020, Slip Opinion No. 2020-Ohio-4775). The final six months of the suspension were stayed on condition that counsel engaged in no further misconduct. See also *R* v *Benson* [1914] AD 357 (Appellate Division of the Supreme Court of South Africa) where counsel for the defence in a South African case was fined for contempt after refusing to follow a direction by the magistrate not to shout at the witness he was cross-examining. His conduct "terrorised the witness. . . . He had shouted spasmodically for seven hours".

pretty pictures to illustrate my points." In an application to the State Supreme Court, Mr Anderson stated: "I'm convinced that with the passing of each so-called 'fart' I dispense more integrity and legal competence than is possessed by all the folks on the panel combined."[141]

A calm and polite advocate is more likely to be a successful advocate.[142] In 1921, Chief Justice Harris for the Supreme Court of Nova Scotia, when fining a barrister $100 for contempt of court, pointed out that "[i]n almost every case we hear there are two barristers, and one of them must be on the losing side; and it would be intolerable if the loser in each case should write an insulting and abusive letter to the Court".[143]

[141] *The North Carolina State Bar* v *Michael J Anderson* (Complaint before the Disciplinary Hearing Commission of the North Carolina State Bar, 16 October 2015). See also *American Bar Association Journal*, posted 3 November 2015. The disciplinary proceedings were stayed because of Mr Anderson's disability: *The North Carolina State Bar* v *Michael J Anderson* (Disciplinary Hearing Commission of the North Carolina State Bar, March 2016).

[142] A calm response to a rude judge was given by Judah Benjamin, counsel who came to this country after playing a prominent role on the Confederate side in the US Civil War. He became pre-eminent at the London commercial bar. In 1881, appearing in the Appellate Committee of the House of Lords, he stated a proposition of law to which Lord Chancellor Selborne responded, in a low voice, "Nonsense". Benjamin "stopped his argument, tied up his brief, bowed and left the House [of Lords]. The next day a conciliatory message was sent to him, and the incident was closed": Professor Arthur L Goodhart *Five Jewish Lawyers of the Common Law* (1949), pp. 13–14.

[143] *In Re O S Miller* 54 NSR (Nova Scotia Reports) 529 (1921). Counsel should also not insult the foreman of the jury during submissions: see

However objectionable the judge, counsel should not make a submission threatening to "settle with him outside", as happened in North Dakota in 1898.[144] Avoiding rudeness to the court is essential, but it may require exceptional self-control. Counsel may find it very hard not to respond in kind if the judge tells him during a hearing, as occurred in Michigan in 1982, "whether your client is guilty or innocent, *you're a despicable son of a bitch*" (the emphasis is in the law report).[145] In Florida in 2014, Judge John C. Murphy told the public defender, "If you want to fight, let's go out back and I'll just beat your ass".[146]

ex parte Pater 5 B & S 299, 300 (1864) recording that counsel for the defendant told the jury, "I thank God that there is more than one juryman to determine whether the prisoner stole the property with which he is charged, for if there were only one, and that one the foreman . . . there is no doubt what the result would be".

144 *State* v *Crum* 74 NW 992 (1898) (Supreme Court of North Dakota).

145 *In the Matter of Marvin F Frankel* 323 NW 2d 911 (1982) (Supreme Court of Michigan). Note also the comments of Judge William B Raines of Cook County, Illinois about counsel, Jennifer Bonjean: "Can you imagine waking up next to her every day?" The judge made his comments to counsel appearing in another case later in the day on which Ms Bonjean had participated in an acrimonious hearing in his court. The judge had not realised that his comments were being broadcast on YouTube: see *American Bar Association Journal*, posted 18 January 2022.

146 In 2015, the Florida Supreme Court removed Judge John C Murphy from judicial office because of this incident in his Brevard County courtroom in 2014. During proceedings in the criminal case, he threatened violence against an assistant public defender for not complying with a judicial direction to sit down ("You know if I had a rock, I would throw it at you right now"). When defence counsel, Andrew Weinstock, responded "I have a right to stand and represent

Defence counsel did well to control herself when Judge Ian Alexander QC, presiding at a jury trial at Northampton Crown Court in 2008 of a man accused of dangerous driving, sent her a note on the second morning of the hearing. The judge's note to counsel was headed "6 P's" and stated: "Prior Planning Prevents Piss Poor Performance." Lord Justice Latham, for the Court of Appeal, said this was "wholly inappropriate". Even if the judge thought that the young barrister might have conducted the trial differently, "that was not the way to express himself. It can have had nothing but a detrimental effect on the confidence" of counsel. For that and other reasons the appeal against conviction was allowed.[147] The Court of Appeal would not say today, as it did in 1967, that "[d]iscourtesy, even gross discourtesy, to counsel, however unfortunate, cannot by itself be any ground for quashing a conviction".[148]

Counsel may need to pursue in the appeal court complaints about judicial rudeness or other misconduct. In 2014, the Court of Appeals of Maryland suspended Judge

my clients", the judge replied by saying "If you want to fight, let's go out back, and I'll just beat your ass". Counsel then walked out of the court followed by the judge and there was a scuffle. The Florida Supreme Court stated: "Judge Murphy's grievous misconduct became a national spectacle [because the proceedings had been recorded and were available on YouTube] and an embarrassment to Florida's judicial system". See *American Bar Association Journal*, posted 17 December 2015 and *Inquiry Concerning a Judge: Re John C Murphy* (Supreme Court of Florida, 17 December 2015).

147 *R* v *Dean Cole* [2008] EWCA Crim 3234.

148 *R* v *Ptohopoulos* (1968) 52 Cr App Rep 47, 50 (Salmon LJ for the Court of Appeal). (The appeal was allowed on another ground.)

Lynn Stewart Mays of the Baltimore City Circuit from the Bench for five days and required her to complete a two-year monitoring period for her incivility to those appearing in her court. She told one advocate that she did not want to hear any more submissions from him "because you're going to lose. . . . You know why? One, I'm the judge. Two, I'm the judge. Three, I'm the judge".[149]

When I began in practice at the Bar in 1980, it was common for judges to make very clear what they thought of submissions which they considered wrong in law. Nowadays, judges tend to be polite – sometimes overpolite – to even the weakest of submissions. The flavour of the old approach is illustrated by Simon Brown – Lord Brown of Eaton-Under-Heywood – in his anecdote of advocacy in the Appellate Committee of the House of Lords in the 1980s. Lord Bridge was "plainly feeling rather guilty at his mauling of junior counsel's argument". As the Committee adjourned for lunch, he asked one of his colleagues, Lord Ackner, whether he had perhaps been too severe with the unfortunate barrister. "Oh no", Lord Ackner replied, "you never actually hit him."[150]

[149] *American Bar Association Journal*, posted 22 October 2014; and *Baltimore Sun*, 22 October 2014.

[150] Simon Brown *Second Helpings* (2021), pp. 81–82. And see also Alan Paterson *Final Judgment: The Last Law Lords and the Supreme Court* (2013), p. 78: in the 1980s "the oral hearings could be somewhat lively if not rather aggressive affairs with inputs from Lords Templeman, Brandon and Bridge which amounted to little less than point-scoring against each other, with counsel sometimes little more than a cipher in the middle".

So my ninth principle of advocacy is refrain from insulting your opponent or the judge, however great the provocation. Though counsel needs also to avoid the excessive familiarity of the advocate appearing before the California Supreme Court who referred to the judges during a hearing as "you guys".[151]

However skilful your advocacy, and however faithfully you follow the principles I have mentioned, there are unwinnable cases where, as Lady Macbeth lamented, "all the perfumes of Arabia will not sweeten this little hand".[152] A good example is the 1977 case in which Lord Hailsham, for the Appellate Committee of the House of Lords, stated that counsel (David Hirst QC, himself later a Court of Appeal judge) "was constrained to argue that the report [of the Law Reform Committee], the authors of which included Lords Pearson and Diplock, Winn and Buckley LJJ, Orr J and the present Vice-Chancellor (Megarry V-C), was an inaccurate representation of the then existing state of the law". Indeed, as Lord Hailsham pointed out, Mr Hirst QC "was himself, as he candidly confessed, signatory to the report".[153] John Roberts was a regular advocate in the US Supreme Court (before his appointment as Chief Justice in 2005). When asked why he had lost a particular case in that court 9–0, he replied "because there were only nine Justices".[154]

151 Bryan A Garner *The Winning Oral Argument* (2009), p. 113.

152 William Shakespeare *Macbeth*, Act 5, Scene 1.

153 *D* v *NSPCC* [1978] AC 171, 227.

154 *National Law Journal* 7 October 2013. The case was *Digital Equipment Corp* v *Desktop Direct* 511 US 863 (1994).

On occasions, counsel recognise the inevitable. In 1765, the Attorney General, Charles Yorke, accepted that the argument advanced against him "was too great a difficulty for him to encounter; and therefore rested the matter where it was, without proceeding any further in his argument".[155] In a 1989 case, Mr Justice Simon Brown noted that counsel's argument "flies in the face of clear Court of Appeal authority directly and indistinguishable in point" and counsel "candidly admitted to sitting transfixed when it came to be cited" by his opponent.[156]

There are cases where counsel puts up a fight but it becomes clear during the hearing that he is not going to win. Gabriel Wendler SC was appearing in the High Court of Australia and the Chief Justice, Sir Anthony Mason, was testing his submissions. Wendler responded, "I believe your Honour may have me on the ropes". The Chief Justice replied, "I have you on the canvas, Mr Wendler, and you're not getting up".[157]

You may think you have a good case, but the judge may then disappoint you. When counsel cited to Baron Bramwell in 1872 an earlier decision of that judge, he responded: "The matter does not appear to me now as it appears to have appeared to me then."[158] I also like the story which Lord Bingham told at the Service of Thanksgiving for

[155] *Money* v *Leach* 3 Burr 1742, 1767–1768; 97 ER 1075, 1088 (1765).
[156] *R* v *Oxford Crown Court ex parte Smith* (1989) 154 JP 422, 427.
[157] Peter Lyons *Advocacy: A Practical Guide* (2019), p. 211.
[158] *Andrews* v *Styrap* 26 LT 704, 706 (1872), cited in R E Megarry *Miscellany-at-Law* (1969), p. 316.

Lord Denning in 1999. Tom Bingham QC was appearing in the Court of Appeal before a court in which Lord Denning, Master of the Rolls, was presiding. Counsel cited in support of his argument the law report of the reasoning of Viscount Simon for seven judges in the Appellate Committee of the House of Lords. Lord Denning was unimpressed. "Oh", he said, "but Lord Simon was very sorry he ever said that. He told me so."[159]

Rarely, and happily much less often nowadays than in the past, the judge may be so perverse that reasoned argument will not assist. In an admittedly extreme example, Mr Justice Byles, a judge in the second half of the nineteenth century, told one of his colleagues that "I always listen with little pleasure to the arguments of counsel whose legs are encased in light grey trousers".[160] Other extraneous considerations may take the judge's eye off the issues in the case. According to the autobiography of retired High Court judge Sir Peter Bristow, his chambers "kept a drawer full of old school and club and regimental ties" in the 1950s and 1960s to impress judges and members of tribunals.[161] Which tells you much about the legal profession of those days. In some jurisdictions, at some times, this point has been taken to extremes. Roy M. Cohn – a corrupt, and well-connected, US lawyer in the 1950s and 1960s – said "I don't want to know

[159] *Service of Thanksgiving for Lord Denning*, Westminster Abbey, 17 June 1999. See *Graya* No. 110, p. 20 (1999).

[160] *Oswald's Contempt of Court* (3rd edition, 1910), p. 58. See also C P Harvey QC *The Advocate's Devil* (1958), p. 34.

[161] *Judge for Yourself* (1986), p. 40.

what the law is, I want to know who the judge is".[162] Abraham H. Hummel, a shyster New York lawyer of the late nineteenth century, claimed to have coined the phrase that there were two kinds of lawyer, "those who knew the law and those who knew the judge".[163]

If you cannot persuade the judge, and you think she has made the wrong decision, save it for the appellate court. Or follow the advice given by Abraham Lincoln: "we can go over to the tavern and, just among ourselves, cuss the judge to our hearts['] content".[164] As to relations with opponents, I have always tried to follow Shakespeare's advice in *The Taming of the Shrew*: "do as adversaries do in law / Strive mightily, but eat and drink as friends".[165] There are, however, some opponents whose conduct makes this very difficult to implement. Very occasionally, I have had a similar reaction to

[162] *Oxford Dictionary of American Legal Quotations* (edited by Fred R Shapiro, 1993), p. 205.

[163] Richard H Rovere *Howe and Hummel* (1947), p. 105.

[164] Dan Abrams and David Fisher *Lincoln's Last Trial* (2018), p. 48. cf Justice Robert H Jackson of the US Supreme Court on "the country lawyer". He "would fight the adverse party, and fight his counsel, fight every hostile witness, and fight the court, fight public sentiment, fight any obstacle to his client's success. He never quit. . . . He moved for new trials, he appealed; and if he lost out in the end, he joined the client at the tavern in damning the judge – which is the last rite in closing an unsuccessful case, and I have officiated in many": cited in *Oxford Dictionary of American Legal Quotations* (edited by Fred R Shapiro, 1993), p. 273.

[165] William Shakespeare *The Taming of the Shrew*, Act 1, Scene 2. In Scott Turow's *The Last Trial* (2020), pp. 415–416, Sandy Stern reflects that "much of his joy in the practice of law has been palling around with other attorneys, despite the vexation he's felt with difficult opponents".

that of Marcia Clark, lead prosecutor in the O. J. Simpson case, concerning one of her opponents, Johnnie Cochran: "I just shook my head and thought, 'I've lost all my respect for you, Johnnie. You're a two-faced, hypocritical bastard.'"[166]

The nine principles of advocacy I have discussed – I have one more to come – are all variants on a theme: you are trying to persuade the judge, so do all you can not to irritate her, whether by inadequate preparation, rambling or unresponsive argument, or in any other way.[167] Using these basic principles, the advocate seeks to reinforce any sympathy the judge may have for the client's position or, if the judge is unsympathetic, to make the unthinkable into the imaginable and then into the obvious. Lawyers often fail to appreciate that good advocacy demands as much listening as speaking. Listening to what interests and concerns the judge, and what the other side are saying and indeed not saying.[168]

None of this guarantees that your advocacy will attain the heights attributed to the nineteenth-century advocate, James Scarlett (later Lord Abinger): that he "had invented a

[166] Marcia Clark (with Teresa Carpenter) *Without a Doubt* (1997), p. 210.

[167] See Mr Justice Joseph W Quinn (of the Ontario Superior Court of Justice), "A Judge's Views: Things Lawyers Do to Annoy Judges; Things They Do to Impress Judges" (Ontario Bar Association, 10 February 2012).

[168] Lord Birkett *Six Great Advocates* (1961), pp. 70–71: Sir Charles Russell QC "possessed that quality of the great advocate which appreciates the significance and meaning of everything that goes on in court, whether it is some slight stir in the jury box, some surprising turn in the evidence, some word from the judge indicating a view, some action of his opponent, or some sudden change of expression on the face of a witness".

machine by the secret use of which in court he could always make the head of a judge nod assent to his propositions".[169] But these principles may help.

However much preparation counsel undertakes, and however experienced and skilful the advocate, his courtroom performance will inevitably leave room for improvement. Robert H. Jackson wrote that as Solicitor General of the United States in the 1930s he made three arguments in every case: first, the argument he planned ("logical, coherent, complete"), second, the argument he actually presented ("incoherent, disjointed, disappointing"), and thirdly, "the utterly

[169] John Lord Campbell *Lives of the Lord Chancellors* (5th edition, 1868), volume 8, p. 281n. See also Quintilian *The Orator's Education*, Book 10, chapter 1 (edited and translated by Donald A Russell, 2001), p. 313 on the skills of Cicero: "Who had ever such a gift of charm? You believe him to be winning by consent what he is really extorting by force; and when he sweeps the judge along with his violence, the judge feels not that he is being hijacked, but that he is going along of his own accord. Indeed such is the authority in everything Cicero says that one is ashamed to disagree. Instead of the partisanship of an advocate, he displays the trustworthiness of a witness or a judge." Also impressive was the skill of Trachalus, as described by Quintilian (Book 12, chapter 5, p. 249): he was speaking before one tribunal and three other tribunals were in session, with "total uproar everywhere", but "he could nevertheless be heard and understood and (a thing particularly galling to the other pleaders) actually applauded in all four Tribunals". The *Dictionary of National Biography* (edited by Sidney Lee, 1897), volume 49, p. 190 describes the skills of Sir Samuel Romilly (1757–1818) at the Bar: he "marshalled his premises and deduced his conclusions with mathematical precision, and his diction was as chaste as his logic was cogent. The unerring instinct with which he detected, and the unfailing felicity with which he exposed a fallacy, united to no small powers of sarcasm and invective, made him formidable in reply".

devastating argument that I thought of after going to bed that night".[170] Lord Justice Stephenson noted for the Court Appeal in 1984 that "the history of judicial decisions is littered with cases in which points that appear later to be obvious have not been taken, even by the most eminent counsel, for reasons which are not clear – it may be from mere human fallibility".[171] One such counsel was Alfred Denning. In a 1951 judgment, Lord Justice Denning said in his disarming manner: "It is unfortunate that the principle which I have enunciated was not drawn to the attention of the court in [earlier proceedings] but that was my fault, because I was counsel in the case."[172]

It is an occupational hazard of being an advocate that you may know about law but little else. As in David Sipress' cartoon in the *New Yorker* of the lawyer standing on the beach with his son, and responding to the boy: "I don't know about tides. What about torts? I know about torts."[173] There is also a danger that a lifetime of advocacy stunts the ability to make judgments of your own. You so focus on how the case can best be put, and what are the strengths and weaknesses of the opposing side, that you find it difficult to come to a decision. According to his biographer, Sir Edward Marshall

[170] Robert H Jackson "Advocacy before the Supreme Court: Suggestions for Effective Presentation", 37 *American Bar Association Journal* 862 (1951), cited in *Oxford Dictionary of American Legal Quotations* (edited by Fred R Shapiro, 1993), p. 11.

[171] *Bonalumi* v *Secretary of State for the Home Department* [1985] QB 675, 682.

[172] *Cassidy* v *Ministry of Health* [1951] 2 KB 343, 363.

[173] *New Yorker* 8 March 2021.

Hall "was without settled convictions on any subject".[174] John Mortimer's Horace Rumpole reflects that he "had spent my whole life being other people, safe blowers, fraudsmen, a few rather gentle murderers. I'd had remarkably little time to be Rumpole".[175] Those who argue for a living are at risk of arguing as their hobby, or indeed as the governing trait of their personality.

For such reasons Lord MacMillan, a Lord of Appeal, suggested in 1937 that as the professional skills of the advocate develop, "this tends to disqualify him for the other spheres of intellectual or practical activity".[176] I fear there is some truth in this – though, of course, much to be said for the opposing view. I will, nevertheless, in my second and third chapters, attempt to arrive at some conclusions of my own about the morality of advocacy and the future of advocacy.

[174] Edward Marjoribanks *The Life of Sir Edward Marshall Hall* (1929), p. 58.

[175] John Mortimer "Rumpole and the Learned Friends" in *The First Rumpole Omnibus* (1983), p. 167. See also Philip Ziegler *Olivier* (2013) at p. 190: "Scratch an actor and you find an actor, [Laurence] Olivier was accustomed to remark".

[176] Lord MacMillan "The Ethics of Advocacy" in *Law and Order* (1937), p. 197. Harold Laski wrote to Justice Oliver Wendell Holmes of the US Supreme Court in 1927 that Mr Justice Roche had said to him, and Laski agreed, that most judges "were vaccinated against the dangers of speculation by their careers at the bar": *Holmes-Laski Letters* (edited by Mark DeWolfe Howe, abridged by Alger Hiss, 1963), volume 2, p. 141 (20 March 1927). Note also that Roy Jenkins, a great politician of the late twentieth century, was correct in stating that "clever, successful lawyers, as there are many examples to show, can be sparingly endowed with general intellectual equipment": *Mr Balfour's Poodle* (1989 edition), p. 240.

Principle 10: When You Have Made Your Points, Sit Down

My tenth and final principle of advocacy is that the advocate must be careful not to go on for too long. Lengthy submissions are not better submissions. You need to make the relevant points, but judges are busy people and courts welcome a presentation that is efficient in its use of time. Quintilian advised that a "useful way of exciting attention is to make the judges think that we shall not detain them long".[177] He knew, as is still an essential truth of advocacy, that "the judge is in a hurry to get to the crux of the matter".[178]

In an admittedly extreme example, Sir Arthur Irvine QC, Solicitor General 1966–1970, is said to have made a closing speech to the jury on behalf of the prosecution in one criminal trial which consisted entirely of the words, "Well, he did it, didn't he?"[179] The obituary of Dan Hollis QC recalled that he made an even shorter closing speech for the defence in another case. He "simply shrugged his shoulders and then sat down again", conveying to the jury that no-one could possibly convict on that evidence.[180] Leave them

[177] Quintilian *The Orator's Education*, Book 4, chapter 1 (edited and translated by Donald A Russell, 2001), pp. 195–197.

[178] Quintilian *The Orator's Education*, Book 4, chapter 5 (edited and translated by Donald A Russell, 2001), p. 303.

[179] *New Law Journal*, 21 February 1992, p. 229.

[180] *The Times* 17 November 2016. In *Ystradyfodwg and Pontypridd Main Sewerage Board* v *Bensted* [1907] AC 264, 268, Lord Herschell said: "the Attorney-General [Sir J Lawson Walton] in the course of exactly seven minutes appeared to me to dispose of the whole day's argument with which we had been entertained".

wanting more is the principle applied by entertainers appearing at the Glasgow Empire and it should be borne in mind by advocates appearing in courts of law.[181]

A great American advocate of the mid-twentieth century, John W. Davis, advised that when you have said what you need to say, "Sit down".[182]

[181] Many judges have expressed to themselves complaints of the sort recorded in his diary by one of the British judges, Lord Birkett, at the Nuremberg War Crimes Tribunal: "[W]ith complete murder in my heart I am compelled to sit in suffering silence, whilst the maddening, toneless, insipid, flat, depressing voice drones on in endless words which have quite lost all meaning": H Montgomery Hyde *Norman Birkett: The Life of Lord Birkett of Ulverston* (1964), p. 506.

[182] John W Davis "The Argument of an Appeal", 26 *American Bar Association Journal* 895, 898 (1940).

2

The Morality of Advocacy

In 2006, a New York lawyer, Eddie Hayes, wrote an entertaining autobiography, entitled *Mouthpiece*. The novelist Tom Wolfe, in his Introduction to the book, explained that in the 1990s and the early years of this century, Hayes was the "go-to guy" of the New York Bar. There were three words uttered by those facing legal difficulties in New York: "Get me Hayes."

Those of you aspiring to be the "go-to guy" of Gray's Inn will be interested in the advice given by Hayes to his readers. According to Hayes, a lawyer needs to get money up-front from clients while they are "still crying". It is important, said Hayes, that you telephone "every single client every single night, always between eleven and twelve o'clock" so that the last thing on their minds before going to sleep is "Eddie Hayes is thinking about me" – though there is, I suppose, a risk that the client's thoughts at that time of night may be, "Why did that idiot lawyer wake me up just as I was falling asleep?"

Other principles set out by Hayes include that if the client asks why you are charging them such high fees, you should make a "shoe speech" in which you point to your custom-made shoes and announce, "If I lose your case, I got to go back to cheap shoes. And I ain't. . . . And you ain't going to jail". Hayes concludes that to succeed as counsel, you must be willing "to get hurt more and also to hurt more people in the process".

These are not principles to be found in the Code of Conduct for the Bar of England and Wales (or Northern Ireland or Scotland). But what is most striking about the professional ethics of Eddie Hayes is that, for all the bluster and aggression, he proudly states that, "like everybody else", he "wouldn't represent child molesters or rapists" because "I didn't like that".[1]

I am often asked – more, I should emphasise, by friends than by judges – "How can you act for such terrible people?" In this chapter I want to address why a barrister is not, and must not be, a "don't go-to guy" for particular types of potential client.

The fundamental task of the advocate is to be argumentative, inquisitive, indignant, flattering or apologetic – as the occasion demands[2] – and always as persuasive as

[1] Edward Hayes with Susan Lehman *Mouthpiece: A Life In – and Sometimes Just Outside – the Law* (2006), pp. viii, 58, 97, 102, 105, 110, 125, 134. Hayes says at p. 137 that he was the model for the lawyer Tommy Killian in Tom Wolfe's *The Bonfire of the Vanities*. See also Tom Wolfe's Introduction at p. xii. Note also the advice from Roy Grutman, another prominent US lawyer, in Roy Grutman and Bill Thomas *Lawyers and Thieves* (1990), p. 51: he gives all new clients "a simple stress test. First I ask them to tell me everything they can about themselves and their case; then, using that information, I hit them with a barrage of insults and sarcasm". Unsurprisingly, "some break down, go home and never come back".

[2] As Quintilian advised, *The Orator's Education*, Book 12, chapter 10 (edited and translated by Donald A Russell, 2001), p. 321, you may, depending on the context, need to "speak gravely, severely, pungently, vehemently, energetically, copiously, bitterly or again affably, quietly, simply, flatteringly, gently [sweetly], briefly, wittily".

possible, on behalf of the person who pays for his voice and brain. The advocate earns her living propounding views to which she does not necessarily subscribe, on behalf of clients for whom she may feel admiration, indifference or contempt, or whose conduct or behaviour in the litigation or generally may please, offend or even outrage her. Counsel's feelings, positive or negative, are irrelevant. You are paid to do a job, like the surgeon operating on a patient or a taxi-driver conveying a passenger, which does not depend on, and should not be influenced by, your views of the client or the conduct of which they are accused. Counsel performs her function without regard to whether appearing on behalf of this client, or making these submissions, will make her popular or the subject of Twitter, or other, abuse.[3]

Many clients tell lies to their advocate, to the judge and, on occasions, to themselves. Counsel should certainly advise the client as to the strengths and weaknesses of the civil or criminal proceedings in which they are involved.[4] The duties of counsel include, as Lord Justice Lawton observed in the Court of Appeal in 1973, giving advice "to save their

[3] Alan Dershowitz has rightly complained that some criminal lawyers in the USA "consult with public relations experts before they take on a controversial client": Alan M Dershowitz *Reasonable Doubt* (1996), p. 158. Or they consider what their other clients may think of them being associated with a particular defendant or litigant.

[4] The obituary of Sir Joseph Cantley, a High Court Judge 1965–1985, noted that he was "noticeably less successful as a Queen's Counsel . . . in the 1950s . . . partly because his blunt, and often unpalatable, advice to . . . clients reduced the volume of leaders' briefs that came his way": *The Times* 11 January 1993.

clients from their own stupidity and folly".[5] But if the client insists, then no matter how unpromising the raw material, irrespective of the antipathy of the judge, and regardless of the views of the public, the task of the advocate in court is to put the case for her client as persuasively as possible.

This may require considerable ingenuity. In 2017, Harland Braun, lawyer for the film director Roman Polanski, was seeking to persuade a Los Angeles Court to guarantee that his client would not serve jail time if he returned to the United States to face sentencing for fleeing the jurisdiction forty years earlier in 1977 after pleading guilty to having sex with a thirteen-year-old girl. Braun told the judge that "Mr Polanski was as justified in fleeing this court's illegal conduct as he was to flee the Germans who invaded Poland".[6]

[5] *R* v *King and Simkins* (1973) 57 Cr App Rep 696, 701. See also Jonathan Sumption *Cursed Kings: The Hundred Years War (volume 4)* (2015), p. 51: King Henry IV was advised by his lawyers that he had no answer to French demands under the terms of the Treaty of Paris and so "[l]ike many difficult clients he looked for more congenial advice elsewhere".

[6] *The Times* 18 April 2017. There are many other examples of effusive advocacy for well-known clients in difficult circumstances. Tom Cunningham acted for Anna Nicole Smith, a former stripper who married an oil billionaire in 1994 when she was twenty-six years old and he was eighty-nine. In support of his client's claim for US$800 million, half of the estate of the late J Howard Marshall, Mr Cunningham commented, "This is not about a gold-digger sucking money. This is about a relationship that was very profound": *The Independent* 29 September 2000. Thomas Mesereau, defence attorney for Michael Jackson on charges of child abuse, stated that "[t]his case is about one thing only. It's about the dignity, the integrity, the decency, the honour, the charity, the innocence and the vindication of a wonderful human being": *The Times* 1 May 2004. On the sacking of Mr Jackson's previous

The advocate's role is to advance one point of view, irrespective of its weaknesses. He must seek to undermine other interests, whatever their merits. The function of the advocate, as Justice Felix Frankfurter of the US Supreme Court understood, "is not to enlarge the intellectual horizon. His task is to seduce, to seize the mind for a predetermined end, not to explore paths to truth".[7] With rare exceptions, "the orator", as Socrates emphasised, "does not teach juries and other bodies about right and wrong – he merely persuades them".[8] Subject to important limits, to which I will come – for example, counsel must not mislead the court – the advocate argues her client's case; she does not judge it. Right and wrong are left for the judge or jury to

lawyers, see Chapter 1 at n. 53. Gerry Spence, representing Imelda Marcos on charges of racketeering and fraud, told a New York jury that although his client was a "world-class shopper", she was also "a world-class decent human being" whose only crime was "loving her husband for 35 years". She was acquitted. See *The Independent* 28 June 1990 and 3 July 1990. After her acquittal, Mrs Marcos held a party for the jury and entertained them with her rendition of "God Bless America": *The Times* 17 July 1990. In 2007, Paris Hilton was sentenced to forty-five days in jail for driving her car in knowing violation of the terms of her probation for an earlier drink driving offence. Her defence counsel, Howard Weitzman, told the press: "I'm shocked, I'm surprised and really disheartened in the system that I've worked in for close to 40 years": *American Bar Association Journal*, posted 5 May 2007.

7 Felix Frankfurter "Mr Justice Jackson", 68 *Harvard Law Review* 937, 939 (1955). The function of the advocate "is to win a particular case before a particular tribunal for a particular client": Karl N Llewellyn "A Lecture on Appellate Advocacy", 29 *University of Chicago Law Review* 627, 629 (1962), cited in Bryan A Garner *The Winning Oral Argument* (2009), p. 9.

8 Plato *Georgias* (translated by Walter Hamilton, 1960), p. 32.

decide. Politely though the task should be performed, many barristers spend much of their working day accusing respectable members of the community of being liars. In a James Thurber cartoon in *The New Yorker* in 1935,[9] counsel, holding on to a kangaroo, asks the witness – "Perhaps *this* will refresh your memory?"

These principles of advocacy have long been controversial. In the fifth century BC, a character in one of Aristophanes' plays pointed out that with the aid of rhetoric, the weaker argument "can always win the debate".[10] Quintilian in the first century AD noted that critics attack oratory because "[i]t is eloquence, they argue, that snatches criminals from punishment, conduces sometimes by its deception to the condemnation of the innocent, leads deliberations astray".[11] Bassanio, in Shakespeare's *The Merchant of Venice*, asks: "In law, what plea so tainted and

[9] *New Yorker* 6 April 1935.

[10] Aristophanes *Clouds*, lines 115–117 (translated by Stephen Halliwell, 2015), p. 25.

[11] *The Orator's Education*, Book 2, chapter 16 (edited and translated by Donald A Russell, 2001), p. 371. Quintilian's mocking answer, chapter 16, at p. 373 was: "Let us have nothing to do with food: it often causes illness. Let us never go indoors: the roof sometimes falls on the people inside. Never let a sword be made for a soldier: a robber can use it." However, Quintilian was concerned – see Book 11, chapter 1, pp. 197–199 – that "if the power of eloquence proves to have put weapons into the hands of evil, there would be nothing more ruinous for public or private life". He feared that, in teaching the principles of oratory, he "would serve humanity very badly if what I am doing is to provide these arms not for the soldier, but for the brigand". Quintilian added at Book 12, chapter 7, p. 259: "the person whom we want as an orator ought not to be defending a cause which he knows to be unjust".

corrupt / But, being season'd with a gracious voice, / Obscures the show of evil?"[12]

In the nineteenth century, Jeremy Bentham complained that if a criminal has committed a theft, someone who helps him to escape will be prosecuted and convicted as an accomplice, but "[w]hat the non-advocate is hanged for, the advocate is paid for, and admired".[13] For John Stuart Mill, advocacy was a disreputable profession because the advocate "hires himself out to do injustice or frustrate justice with his tongue". Mill complained that by "putting on a wig and gown, a man obtains, and on the most important of all occasions, an exemption" from truth and justice. The advocate persuades "a deluded jury into a verdict in direct opposition to the strongest evidence" and "throw[s] the faculties of a bona fide witness into a state of confusion", causing him "to be taken for a perjurer and as such disbelieved".[14]

The skills of some eminent lawyers have highlighted the moral ambivalence of advocacy. It was said of the

[12] William Shakespeare *The Merchant of Venice*, Act 3, Scene 2.

[13] *Works of Jeremy Bentham* (edited by John Bowring, 1843), volume 6, p. 350.

[14] "Remarks by the Editor", John Stuart Mill, in "Rationale of Judicial Evidence" in *Works of Jeremy Bentham* (edited by John Bowring, 1843), volume 7, p. 479. On Mill's role as the editor of Bentham's "Rationale of Judicial Evidence", see John Stuart Mill *Autobiography* (1971), pp. 69–71. A similar indictment of the advocate to that advanced by Bentham and Mill can be found in Jonathan Swift *Gulliver's Travels* (1726), "A Voyage to the Houyhnhnms", chapter 5: "there was a society of men among us, bred up from their youth in the art of proving by words multiplied for the purpose, that white is black, and black is white, according as they are paid".

American lawyer Rufus Choate in 1859 that because of his courtroom skills, he "made it safe to murder, and of [his] health thieves asked before they began to steal".[15] More recently, the Californian defence attorney Leslie Abrahamson was described by one of her clients, a contract killer, as "so good [that] for a while there she even had me believing I didn't do it".[16] Critics of the ethics of advocacy can point to the memoirs of Sir Henry Hawkins (appointed to the Bench in 1876 after a successful career at the Bar). He recalled that "[m]y greatest delight, perhaps, was the obtaining [of] an acquittal of someone whose guilt nobody could doubt".[17] In his 1946 memoirs, Travers Humphreys recalled defence counsel Willie Willis saying to his client that he would do his best for him but the client needed to assure him of one thing. "Certainly Mr Willis, what is it?" "Promise me . . . that if I get you off this time you will never do it again".[18]

[15] See Fred R Shapiro, *Oxford Dictionary of American Legal Quotations* (1993), p. 281. A similar phrase was used by the District Attorney, Robert Crowe, in the Leopold and Loeb murder trial. He referred in his closing speech to defence counsel Clarence Darrow as "[t]he distinguished gentleman whose profession it is to protect murder in Cook County, and concerning whose health thieves inquire before they go to commit crime": Robert Furneaux *Courtroom USA, volume* 2 (1963), p. 51 and John Farrell *Clarence Darrow: Attorney for the Damned* (2011), p. 356.

[16] Mick Brown *Tearing Down the Walls of Sound: The Rise and Fall of Phil Spector* (2008), p. 435.

[17] *The Reminiscences of Sir Henry Hawkins* (edited by Richard Harris KC, 1904), p. 94.

[18] Travers Humphreys *Criminal Days* (1946), p. 105. In the television comedy *Hancock's Half Hour* broadcast on 2 December 1957, *The Crown* v *James (S)* (written by Alan Simpson and Ray Galton), Tony

Literature is full of advocates who are portrayed as amoral. Tolstoy describes what happens after an old lady has lost her case in court because of the "genius of a lawyer" for the other side:

> Following the old lady out of the door of the Civil Court, starched shirt-front resplendent under his low-cut waistcoat, a self-satisfied look on his face, hurried the famous advocate who had fixed matters in such a way that the old lady with the flowers lost all she had, while the smart fellow, his client, for a fee of ten thousand roubles, had got his hands on over a hundred thousand. Aware that all eyes were directed upon him, his whole bearing seemed to say: "Please, I don't need any acts of homage", and quickly made his way through the crowd.[19]

Hancock as an unsuccessful barrister is questioning his client in court: "And what will you do if you get away with it – I mean if you are exonerated?" A medical malpractice lawyer, Robert L McKenna III, who won a case for a defendant doctor in California was (understandably) criticised for boasting to his colleagues, in a video posted on the firm's social media page, that the litigation concerned "a guy that was probably negligently killed, but we kind of made it look like other people did it". Mr McKenna apologised for his "imprecise" remarks which, he said, "might understandably cause confusion for a lay audience unfamiliar with the case at hand and the law in general". See *Los Angeles Times* 6 June 2022 and *American Bar Association Journal*, posted 7 June 2022.

19 Tolstoy *Resurrection* (1899), Part 1, chapter 6. In David Grossman's novel *A Horse Walks into a Bar* (2016), p. 64, Avishai Lazar, formerly a District Court judge, reflects on how he had to retire for saying what he believed, in particular telling a lawyer that "I thought he was the scum of the earth".

The "business" of Anthony Trollope's Mr Chaffanbrass "is to perplex a witness and bamboozle a jury . . . Let him by the use of his high art rescue from the gallows and turn loose upon the world the wretch whose hands are reeking with the blood of father, mother, wife and brother, and you may see Mr Chaffanbrass elated with conscious worth, rub his happy hands with infinite complacency".[20]

For such reasons, the Metropolitan Police Commissioner, Sir Robert Mark, stated in his 1973 BBC Dimbleby Lecture that "Experienced and respected metropolitan detectives can identify lawyers in criminal practice who are more harmful to society than the clients they represent".[21] Some counsel have accepted the force of these arguments and refused to represent clients whom they considered to be guilty of the criminal offence charged or to be seeking to promote an injustice. Chief Justice Hale, in his early years at the Bar in the

[20] *The Three Clerks* (1857), chapter 40. In *Orley Farm* (1862), chapter 18, another Trollope lawyer, Mr (Thomas) Furnival, makes a passionate speech to the jury urging a verdict of not guilty for his client, even though "he knew that she had been guilty". Yet, "the legal world found no fault with Mr Furnival, conceiving that he had done his duty by his client in a manner becoming an English barrister and an English gentleman". And in Trollope's' *Phineas Redux* (1874), chapter 61, Lord Chiltern comments: "I never believe anything that a lawyer says when he has a wig on his head and a fee in his hand. I prepare myself beforehand to regard it all as mere words, supplied at so much the thousand".

[21] *Minority Verdict* (1973, Dimbleby Lecture, BBC Television). See also Mario Puzo *The Godfather* (1969), chapter 1: "A lawyer with his briefcase can steal more than a hundred men with guns". In *The Yale Book of Quotations* (2006), p. 623, the editor, Fred R Shapiro, notes that "This line does not appear in the film *The Godfather*" – or indeed in the sequels.

mid-seventeenth century, would only plead for a party who had right on their side, "for he would assist none in acts of injustice".[22] After securing a not guilty verdict on behalf of a client whom he thought was obviously guilty, one of the Founding Fathers of the USA, Alexander Hamilton, wrote in 1786 that he decided that "I would never again take up a cause in which I was convinced I ought not to prevail".[23]

[22] John Lord Campbell *Lives of the Chief Justices* (3rd edition, 1874), volume 2, pp. 165–166. During his final years on the bench in the early 1730s, Lord Chancellor King "often dozed over his causes", and two eminent counsel, Sir Philip Yorke and Charles Talbot, having presented the opposing arguments, understood which side was right in law and "arranged the minutes of the decrees" accordingly: Edward Foss *Biographia Juridica* (1870), p. 387. Foss observes: "No wonder then that this mode of settling their claims was unsatisfactory to the litigants". See also John Lord Campbell *Lives of the Lord Chancellors* (5th edition, 1868), volume 6, pp. 121–122. Campbell adds at p. 122n that Chief Justice Gibbs told him that when at the Bar in the early years of the nineteenth century, and appearing before a weak judge on the Western Circuit, he insisted on a decision against his client in a civil case "and saved my client the expense of having a verdict in his favour set aside" by an appeal court. In 1989, the prosecutor failed to attend a hearing at the Hendon Magistrates' Court. The defence solicitor, Mr Patrick Cusack, was concerned that his client's case – he was pleading guilty to a motoring offence – would be adjourned, to the client's detriment. So, with the permission of the magistrates, he performed the role of the prosecutor, outlining the facts, and then presented the mitigating circumstances on behalf of his client. The defendant was fined £300 and ordered to perform 200 hours of community service. As Mr Cusack later explained, he did not ask for prosecution costs against himself: *The Independent* 4 August 1989.

[23] Ron Chernow *Alexander Hamilton* (2004), p. 189. Hamilton was a very unusual lawyer: Chernow records at p. 188 that Hamilton's clients' "sole quibble with him is the modesty of the fees that he asks". Nazir Afzhal

Abraham Lincoln refused to take a case where the client had strong arguments in law but no claim in justice or equity. Lincoln told him: "You'll have to get some other fellow to win this case for you. I couldn't do it. All the time while standing talking to that jury I'd be thinking, 'Lincoln, you're a liar', and I believe I should forget myself and say it out loud." Lincoln was described as having "sat as a court of equity in sifting out the cases he would or would not accept, trying them all first in his own 'court of conscience'".[24] William Kunstler, the radical US attorney best known nowadays for acting for the defence in the Chicago 7 trial in 1969,[25] was reported as saying, "I'm not a lawyer for hire. I only defend those I love".[26]

That is not the principle of advocacy which I, and most counsel, apply. If I had confined my advocacy to those

(who served as Chief Crown Prosecutor for Northwest England) said that he had started his career as a defence counsel but had left to join the Crown Prosecution Service in 1991 because, representing an alleged rapist, he decided "I can't do this. Good for people who can and we need people who can do that, but it wasn't for me". See *BBC Website* 1 August 2021 and *The Times* 2 August 2021.

24 Albert A Woldman *Lawyer Lincoln* (1994), pp. 155 and 193. After Lincoln's assassination in 1865, his former law partner, Stephen Logan, said that when Lincoln "believed his client was right, especially in difficult and complicated cases, he was the strongest and most comprehensive reasoner and lawyer he ever met – or if the case was somewhat doubtful but could be decided either way without violating any just, equitable or moral principle, he was very strong – but if he thought his client was wrong he would make very little effort": Dan Abrams and David Fisher *Lincoln's Last Trial* (2018), p. 283.

25 He was portrayed by Mark Rylance in a film about the trial: *The Trial of the Chicago 7* (2020).

26 56 *American Bar Association Journal* 552 (June 1970).

clients I loved, I would have been unemployed for large parts of each year. There are two compelling defences of the morality of advocacy for any client, however unattractive their conduct or cause may be.

The first is that the law provides for someone to decide where legal right and wrong lies, and it is not the advocate.[27] It is the task of the judge or the jury to assess guilt or innocence in a criminal case, and to adjudicate where liability lies in a civil dispute. The role of the advocate is to ensure that when judges and juries come to make up their minds, they are assisted in their difficult task by having the competing arguments on each side put before them as powerfully as possible.

As Sir Thomas Bingham said for the Court of Appeal in 1994, this is an "essentially antagonistic" theory of litigation. Each side "is determined to win, and prepares and presents his case so as to defeat his opponent and achieve a favourable result", and it is "by the clash of competing evidence and argument" that "the judge is best enabled to decide what happened, to formulate the relevant principles of law and to apply those principles to the facts of the case".[28]

[27] John Mortimer *Murderers and Other Friends* (1994), p. 8: the advocate learns "to refrain from judgment. There are plenty of people whose business it is to perform this unpleasant function: judges, juries and, perhaps, God. The defender's task is to listen and suspend disbelief".

[28] *Ridehalgh* v *Horsefield* [1994] Ch 205, 224. See *Lowdon* v *US* 149 F 673, 676 (1906) (US Court of Appeals, Fifth Circuit): "the experience of all civilized countries shows that a trained body of men, advocates and judges, each class performing its respective duties, is required even to approximate success in the establishment of truth". And see William

This is an ancient concept of fairness. In the play *Eumenides* by Aeschylus, first performed in around 450 BC, the goddess Athena sits in judgment on Orestes, who is accused by the Furies of murdering his mother, Clytemnestra. After hearing the allegation, Athena declares: "Two parties are present: I have had only half of the story."[29] The complexity of the case may be revealed only after both sides are heard. When James I decided to act as a judge, he was "so much perplexed when he had heard both sides that he abandoned the trade in despair, saying 'I could get on very well hearing one side only, but when both sides have been heard, by my soul I know not which is right'".[30]

The essential point about the ethics of advocacy was put as well as anyone by Samuel Johnson, as recorded by James Boswell in his *Journal of a Tour to the Hebrides* for 15 August 1773. Dr Johnson said that "a lawyer has no business with the justice or injustice of the cause which he

Blake's *The Marriage of Heaven and Hell* (1790–1793): "Without contraries is no progression". In *Conflicted: Why Arguments Are Tearing Us Apart and How They Can Bring Us Together* (2021), pp. 55–56, Ian Leslie explained that the successful investor, Warren Buffett, advised that when a company is considering a takeover bid for another, it should not just employ consultants to advise on the merits of the deal (and pay them if the deal goes through), but it should also employ consultants to advise against the deal (and pay them only if the deal does not proceed).

29 Aeschylus *Oresteia*: *Eumenides* (edited and translated by Alan H Sommerstein, 2008), p. 409, line 428. See also Aristophanes *The Wasps* (translated by Kenneth McLeish, 1993), lines 724–725: "Never prejudge the issue, they say. / Hear both sides of the argument first."

30 John Lord Campbell *Lives of the Chief Justices* (1874 edition), volume 1, p. 321.

undertakes, unless his client asks his opinion, and then he is bound to give it honestly. The justice or injustice of the cause is to be decided by the judge". He added: "If lawyers were to undertake no causes till they were sure they were just, a man might be precluded altogether from a trial of his claim, though, were it judicially examined, it might be found a very just claim."[31] The same point was put by Thomas Erskine in his defence of Thomas Paine in 1792 on a charge of seditious libel:

> If the advocate refuses to defend from what *he may think* of the charge or of the defence, he assumes the character of a judge; nay, he assumes it before the hour of judgment; and in proportion to his rank and reputation, puts the heavy influence of perhaps a mistaken opinion into the scale against the accused.[32]

[31] Samuel Johnson and James Boswell *The Journal of a Tour to the Hebrides* (edited by Peter Levi, 1984), pp. 168–169.

[32] *R* v *Thomas Paine* (1792) 22 State Trials 358, 412. See also *Johnson* v *Emerson and Sparrow* [1871] LR 6 Ex 329, 367, where Baron Bramwell said that "A man's rights are to be determined by the Court, not by his . . . counsel. . . . A client is entitled to say to his counsel, I want your advocacy, not your judgment; I prefer that of the Court". And see Lord MacMillan "The Ethics of Advocacy" in *Law and Other Things* (1937), p. 171: counsel's "duty is to see that those whose business it is to judge do not do so without first hearing from him all that can possibly be urged on his side". As stated in the *Bar Standards Board Code of Conduct*, Guidance paragraph 6: "Your role when acting as an advocate or conducting litigation is to present your *client's* case, and it is not for you to decide whether your *client's* case is to be believed". In Barbara Demnick's account of justice in North Korea, when a defendant was on trial accused of stealing copper wire, his lawyer offered no defence, telling the court, "I have determined that what the prosecutor says is

There are many historical examples of counsel performing this professional duty in the most difficult of circumstances. One celebrated such case occurred in 1770 in Boston, Massachusetts when the popular desire for independence was held back by British military forces. The thirty-four-year-old old John Adams – a supporter of independence and a future President of the United States – acted as defence counsel for the British captain and soldiers who opened fire on a crowd of demonstrators, killing five of them. He was told that no other lawyer was prepared to defend those accused of the "Boston massacre". So he took the brief, despite incurring, in his words, "a clamour and popular suspicions and prejudices". The captain and six of the eight soldier defendants were acquitted (the other two were convicted of manslaughter). Adams claimed that he lost more than half his law practice but in old age he looked back with justified pride that his role as defence counsel was "one of the best pieces of service I ever rendered my country".[33]

I share Sir Thomas Bingham's view that "the interests of justice are on the whole best served"[34] if a civil dispute or a criminal charge is decided by independent judges and juries who hear argument from both sides. A role model for the advocate is the defence attorney in Jack Ziegler's *New Yorker* cartoon who stands up in court,

true", and his client was led away to be executed: Barbara Demnick *Nothing to Envy* (2010), p. 186.

33 David McCullough *John Adams* (2004), pp. 65–68.

34 *Ridehalgh* v *Horsefield* [1994] Ch 205, 224.

next to his client, a whale, and tells the judge, "Objection, Your Honor. *Alleged* killer whale".[35]

Ensuring that the judge or jury hears both sides so as to improve the prospects of arriving at a legally correct decision is not the only justification for the principles of advocacy. A second justification, which I also find persuasive, is that the rule of law requires that the state does not send people to prison or impose civil liabilities to pay damages or comply with injunctions, or decide a family law or other legal dispute without giving the person concerned the opportunity to be heard, whether or not it makes any difference to the result.

In 1723, Mr Justice Fortescue, in upholding the right of Dr Bentley to a fair hearing before he was deprived of his degree by the University of Cambridge, noted that "even God himself did not pass sentence on Adam before he was called on to make his defence".[36] Of course, God, being omniscient, did not need to hear from Adam before arriving at a just decision.[37] Nevertheless, a fair process values the right to be heard as essential if those who are the subject of adverse decisions, and the community at large, are to have confidence in the legal system and are going to accept the decisions which are made.

Recent judgments of the United Kingdom Supreme Court have rightly emphasised this important justification of

[35] *New Yorker* 26 May 2008. See Bob Mankoff *How about Never – Is Never Good for You? My Life in Cartoons* (2014), pp. 237–238.

[36] *R* v *Chancellor of Cambridge ex parte Bentley* (1723) 2 Ld Ram 1334.

[37] As pointed out by Lord Hoffmann in *Secretary of State for the Home Department* v *AF (No. 3)* [2010] 2 AC 269, paragraph 72.

the duty of the court to ensure a fair hearing.[38] This too is an ancient concept of justice. In Seneca's play *Medea*, written in about 50 AD, Medea complains about the unfairness of Creon's decision to exile her: "he who decides an issue without hearing one side has not been just, however just the decision".[39] Because most (indeed nearly all) defendants and litigants lack the ability personally to put their case to the court coherently and by reference to the relevant legal rules, there needs to be a profession of advocates able and willing to do so. Therefore, as Dr Johnson noted, "A lawyer is to do for his client all that his client might fairly do for himself, if he could".[40]

There are periodic outbursts from those who do not understand, or value, that it is the task of the advocate to present the case for their client, any client, however unattractive it or he may be. In 1975, after the conviction and sentencing of defendants on charges of planting bombs in London and south-east England on behalf of the IRA, the trial judge, Mr Justice Melford Stevenson, criticised some of the defence counsel for acting as "mere loudspeakers of a maladjusted set". The judge added that it was a "sad day for the Bar of England" that his observations had to be made. The Bar Council issued a robust statement in response,

[38] See Lord Reed for the Supreme Court in *R (Osborn)* v *Parole Board* [2014] AC 1115 at paragraphs 66–71 and Lord Kerr and Lady Black for the Supreme Court in *Pathan* v *Secretary of State for the Home Department* [2020] 1 WLR 4506 at paragraphs 124–126.

[39] Seneca *Tragedies: Medea* (edited and translated by John G Fitch, 2002), lines 199–200, p. 363.

[40] Samuel Johnson and James Boswell *The Journal of a Tour to the Hebrides*, 15 August 1773 (edited by Peter Levi, 1984), p. 169.

> to make it clear beyond any doubt that members of the Bar will continue to carry out their duty as counsel for any persons, whosoever they may be and whatever the nature of the crime alleged against them. . . . [I]t will be a sad day for the Bar when any barrister is deterred from doing his duty by any fear of official displeasure or hope for personal advantage. . . . It is not the duty of counsel for the defence to judge the truth of his client's assertions of fact.[41]

These principles need to be articulated from time to time because criticisms of counsel for performing their job continue to be made by people who ought to know better. There have recently been three well-publicised controversies raising this important issue.

The first was when David Perry QC agreed to appear for the prosecution in a politically sensitive public order case in Hong Kong in January 2021. The then Foreign Secretary, Dominic Raab, described his conduct as "pretty mercenary".[42] Baroness Kennedy of the Shaws QC, chair of the International Bar Association's human rights Institute, said that she could not understand "why any reputable British barrister would provide a veneer of respectability to actions which are contrary to democracy and the rule of law".[43]

The answer is that advocates are not "mercenaries" but an indispensable element of the administration of justice. David Perry QC was proposing to act for the prosecution before an independent court in the manner he has done

[41] *The Times* 19 March 1975.

[42] *The Times* 18 January 2021.

[43] *The Times* 14 January 2021.

throughout his career. Indeed, as a prosecutor, he has a special duty to ensure fairness to the defendant.[44] The prosecution was not being brought under the controversial national security laws. I do, of course, understand that there comes a point when a legal system fails to protect the rule of law, the independence of the judiciary and basic human rights, and so no self-respecting lawyer should appear as a prosecutor in cases brought in that legal system. But that was not the case in Hong Kong in January 2021. Indeed, the vast majority of judges and lawyers in Hong Kong (most of them no friends of Beijing) wanted British lawyers such as Mr Perry to maintain involvement in their legal system and not to abandon them, as they believed that this was an important means of trying to ensure that the courts remained independent of government and the rule of law was upheld. Mr Perry returned the brief, citing the criticism he had received and the difficulties in acting because of Covid-19 quarantine regulations in Hong Kong.[45]

The second recent example of a failure to understand the principles of advocacy was the criticism, in January 2021, of my Blackstone Chambers colleague Dinah Rose QC for representing the government of the Cayman Islands in the Judicial Committee of the Privy Council to argue that there is no legal right to same-sex marriage under the Cayman Constitution. Among the critics was Edwin Cameron, a former judge of the South African Constitutional Court,

[44] See nn. 147–149 below.

[45] Press Release by the Government of the Hong Kong Special Administrative Region, 20 January 2021.

who expressed his "distress and dismay" that Ms Rose, who was also President of Magdalen College, Oxford, was presenting in court what he described as a "homophobic case".[46]

Ms Rose was arguing a case, not agreeing with it. The principles of advocacy transcend support for a political cause, even one as important as the promotion of LGBT rights in the Cayman Islands. Some critics argued that, of course, Ms Rose was entitled to argue such a case as a barrister but she could not do so and at the same time perform her duties as head of a college which supported equality. But that again is wrongly to associate the advocate with the views or position of her clients.

The third recent context in which these issues have arisen concerned the appalling Russian invasion of Ukraine in February 2022 and the imposition of sanctions on oligarchs who were personally and financially linked to President Putin. Solicitors and barristers who had advised, or were advising, such individuals were criticised for their "amoral" behaviour.[47] Those critics lost sight of one of the basic pillars of

[46] *The Times* 29 January 2021 and *Cherwell* 27 January 2021. See also Melanie Phillips "Vindictiveness of woke warriors knows no bar", *The Times* 2 February 2021. The Judicial Committee of the Privy Council held that there was no legal right to same-sex marriage under the Constitution of the Cayman Islands: *Day* v *The Government of the Cayman Islands* [2022] UKPC 6.

[47] See Bob Seely MP in the House of Commons, *Hansard* 1 March 2022, columns 974–975, and *The Times* 2 March 2022. *The Times* published an editorial on 21 March 2022 complaining that "lawyers who act for Russian oligarchs in attempting to protect their wealth and reputations are not disinterestedly pursuing justice. They are enriching themselves and their firms by defending the powerful against scrutiny". I represented

the rule of law, which distinguishes our society from Putin's Russia: people are entitled to advice from lawyers on their legal rights and duties, and they are entitled to legal representation in court, however reprehensible their alleged conduct. The principle applies to oligarchs as it does to alleged murderers or paedophiles – and, indeed, those convicted of such offences who are appealing against conviction. Justifiable outrage at the conduct of Putin, and those who support him, should not be allowed to dilute this vital ingredient of a free society, however inconvenient or unpopular it may sometimes be.

The point was eloquently made by the then Justice Minister, Lord Wolfson of Tredegar (a very distinguished commercial law QC before his appointment), in a tweet on 10 March 2022: "The rule of law means that *everyone* [his emphasis] is entitled to a defence, especially those accused of the worst offences. Don't judge a surgeon by their patients, a journalist by their interviewees – or a lawyer by their clients. (Apologies to some former clients)." Regrettably, the Attorney General, Suella Braverman, made no such statement.

I should also mention the sanctions which the People's Republic of China announced it was imposing in June 2021 against four barristers because they had signed an

Arkady Rotenberg (a close associate of President Putin) in 2014–2015 in the Court of Appeal on a sanctions issue in family law proceedings, and I advised in relation to his claim in the General Court of the EU in mid-2015 challenging the sanctions against him, although I did not represent him at the hearing in Luxembourg 2016. I have also acted for a Russian client whose assets were frozen by the United Kingdom Government in April 2022.

opinion addressing alleged human rights violations by China. I mention this, even though it was not concerned with advocacy in court, because the statement by the Bar Council of England and Wales with the Commonwealth Lawyers Association[48] expressing concern about the sanctions drew attention to the Basic Principles on the Role of Lawyers adopted by the Eighth United Nations Congress on the Prevention of Crime and the Treatment of Offenders 1990. Paragraph 18 of those principles states: "Lawyers shall not be identified with their clients or their clients' causes as a result of discharging their functions." And that is the point.

In one of John Mortimer QC's short stories, Horace Rumpole is told by his head of chambers that "old Keith from the Lord Chancellor's office … was surprised at you of all people … defending a wretched Fascist beast". Rumpole replies: "I defend murderers. Doesn't mean I approve of

48 *Bar Council and Commonwealth Lawyers Association joint statement on China sanctions* 22 June 2021. A further example of a failure to understand the duties of lawyers was the comment of Prime Minister Boris Johnson, who accused lawyers representing asylum-seekers of "abetting" the criminal gangs that organised dangerous and illegal Channel crossings. The Bar Council and the Law Society issued a joint statement calling on the Prime Minister to "stop attacks on legal professionals who are simply doing their job": *The Times* 15 June 2022. In rejecting an application to prevent the Home Secretary from removing an asylum-seeker to Rwanda for his claim to be processed there, Lord Reed, President of the Supreme Court, said that "In bringing that application, the appellant's lawyers were performing their proper function of ensuring that their clients are not subjected to unlawful treatment at the hands of the Government": *R (NSK – Iraq)* v *Secretary of State for the Home Department* (14 June 2022).

murder."[49] Rumpole's wife, Hilda, is not persuaded by his defence of advocacy. When Rumpole tells her that the principle of his profession is that "I will accept any client, however repulsive", Hilda responds, "That's not a principle, that's just a way of making money from the most terrible people".[50]

The principle means that however awful the allegations against a potential client, however repulsive they may be, your job as an advocate is to advise and represent them. I would (I hope) have been prepared to defend Adolf Eichmann – convicted in Israel in 1961 and executed in 1962 for war crimes and crimes against humanity, including his role in organising the Holocaust. I would be prepared to give legal advice and to represent President Vladimir Putin – if he were ever to be brought before the International Criminal Court for approving the invasion by Russia of Ukraine and for approving the barbarous methods used in that campaign. To advise and represent such people, or the Moors Murderers or the Boston Strangler, does not connote any degree of sympathy for them, their conduct or their views. Indeed, if they were to ask me, I would tell them so. Giving them legal advice and representing them in court

[49] John Mortimer QC "Rumpole and the Fascist Beast" in *The First Rumpole Omnibus* (1983), p. 280.

[50] John Mortimer "Rumpole and the Bubble Reputation" in *Rumpole and the Age of Miracles* (1988), p. 18. Hilda Rumpole is unpersuaded by the principles of advocacy. "I suppose that if someone murdered *me*, you would defend them?", she asks in John Mortimer "Rumpole and the Way through the Woods" in *Rumpole and the Angel of Death* (1995), p. 64.

simply means a recognition that the proper administration of justice depends on all defendants – and any defendant – having competent counsel.

Judge Jeffreys commented in court in the 1680s to a Mr Wallop, "a gentlemen of eminence at the Bar", that "I observe you are in all these dirty causes".[51] I certainly have been prepared to act in some "dirty causes" and I have done so because I believe that once you start to reject clients associated with controversial views or conduct, people will assume that any client you *do* represent has your approval. Barristers would then be judged by the clientele that we keep and unpopular litigants would find it much more difficult to obtain competent representation.

There is already an unpleasant tendency for counsel to be threatened or abused by opponents of controversial causes. During the case brought by my client Gina Miller, challenging the legality of the decision by Prime Minister Boris Johnson in 2019 to prorogue Parliament for five weeks,[52] I received a number of very angry letters and emails. One correspondent wrote, anonymously, to tell me that I was a "corrupt bastard" and "a liar, and cheat and above all a TRAITOR [his or her capital letters] to this country". That was polite compared to the email I received after the Divisional Court hearing from

[51] John Lord Campbell *Lives of the Lord Chancellors* (5th edition, 1868), volume 4, p. 421. During the Second Reading of the Terrorism Bill in the House of Lords in 2005, Lord Hurd (a former Home Secretary) said that "in my experience, obnoxious people of all descriptions tend to have good lawyers": *Hansard*, House of Lords, 21 November 2005, column 1401.

[52] *R (Miller)* v *Prime Minister* [2020] AC 373.

another anonymous correspondent who told me I was a "dumb c***" who did not "know what democracy is" but "I bet you know what backhanders are". When I forwarded the email to my senior clerk, Gary Oliver, he asked if it was a response from the Supreme Court to our notice of appeal. When I represented in the Supreme Court Shamima Begum (who, at the age of fifteen, had travelled to Syria where she married an ISIS fighter, and who wanted to return to the United Kingdom to challenge the decision of the Secretary of State to revoke her British citizenship), I received some very unpleasant and threatening emails.[53] If advocates were able to pick and choose their clients, they would inevitably be more closely associated with the opinions or conduct of those they represent, and such abuse would become much more frequent and even more extreme.

The Code of Conduct for barristers imposes two basic and closely linked requirements. The first is a requirement not to discriminate between clients, by which it means something broader than not treating potential clients less favourably because of their race or sex or by reference to other prohibited grounds. The non-discrimination requirement is that a barrister cannot refuse to represent a potential client "on the ground that the nature of the case is objectionable to you or to any section of the public", or "on the ground that the conduct, opinions or beliefs of the prospective client are unacceptable to you or to any section of the public".[54] As the

[53] *R (Begum)* v *Special Immigration Appeals Commission* [2021] 2 WLR 556.

[54] *Bar Standards Board Code of Conduct*, Rule C28.

Code of Conduct explains, any such discrimination is "inherently inconsistent with your role in upholding access to justice and the rule of law".[55]

The second and linked requirement under the Bar Code of Conduct concerns the so-called "cab rank rule". It provides that a barrister may not decline to accept instructions because of the identity of the client, the nature of the case, or "any belief or opinion which you have formed as to the character, reputation, cause, conduct, guilt or innocence of the client".[56] There may be other reasons for rejecting a potential client: if you do not practice in the relevant area of law, you are too busy with other cases, or you have a conflict of interest.[57] But the apparent strength of the case against the client is not a permissible reason for refusing to act for him.[58]

[55] *Bar Standards Board Code of Conduct*, Guidance gC88.

[56] *Bar Standards Board Code of Conduct*, Rule C29.d.

[57] The Code of Conduct does not impose the cab-rank rule in relation to "any foreign work": Rule C30.5. But the requirement not to discriminate under Rule C28 applies whether the work is domestic or foreign.

[58] In 2009, in San Diego, public defender Jeffrey Martin represented a very obnoxious client, Weusi McGowan, on charges of robbery and residential burglary. After the judge refused an application by McGowan that he be allowed to defend himself, McGowan produced in court a plastic bag filled with human excrement, and smeared it on his lawyer's hair and face, and then threw the rest at the jury. The judge declared a mistrial: *American Bar Association Journal*, posted 27 January 2009. After being represented by a new lawyer, McGowan was convicted of the substantive charges, and of assault on his lawyer, and sentenced to thirty-one years in prison: *The San Diego Union-Tribune* 26 October 2009. Note the unusual reason given by Edward Genson for withdrawing from representing Rod Blagojevich, the Governor of Illinois who was

So the advocate is and must be a taxi-cab, prepared to assist any client, irrespective of their merits – although the analogy is far from perfect because the passenger is normally required to accept the first taxi in the queue at the cab-rank. Barristers speak of a taxi-cab, but I prefer the judicial description recorded in the obituary of Michael Lavery QC in *The Times* in 2019. He was appearing in the Court of Appeal, arguing a point of law. "But Mr Lavery", said one of the judges, "you were here yesterday arguing the opposite." Lavery replied, "My Lord, I am simply a taxi for hire". The judge responded, "More a limousine, Mr Lavery".[59]

The limits of the professional obligation should also be noted. There is no professional duty to like an obnoxious client or to maintain other than a professional contact with them. After Marshall Hall secured an acquittal for a defendant accused of disreputable conduct, the client asked to shake his counsel's hand. Marshall Hall refused: "No, that is not included in the etiquette of the Bar, or in the brief-fee."[60]

Critics[61] have pointed out that the non-discrimination and cab-rank principles apply to a very small

accused of trying to sell the US Senate seat vacated by Barack Obama when he became President. Genson told reporters, "I never require a client to do what I say, but I do require them to at least listen": *The Guardian* 26 January 2009. Blagojevich was convicted, and sentenced to fourteen years in prison. He was pardoned by President Trump in 2020: *The Guardian* 22 February 2020.

[59] *The Times* 28 May 2019.

[60] Thomas Grant *Court Number One* (2019), p. 406, n. 6.

[61] See, in particular, John Flood and Morten Hviid *The Cab Rank Rule: Its Meaning and Purpose in the New Legal Services Market* (Report for the Legal Services Board, 2013).

proportion of the legal profession since solicitors have no such obligations, the exceptions allow ample opportunity for a barrister who does not want to take a case to decline to do so, there is no evidence to suggest that without the rules clients would be unable to secure representation,[62] and there have rarely been disciplinary findings against barristers for breaching the principles.[63]

But this is to miss the point. If barristers are to justify their role on the basis that we are speaking for the client, any client, irrespective of their character, conduct or views, we do so to promote the rule of law, and so we should not be criticised for such professional association, we cannot then also claim the privilege of rejecting clients when their alleged behaviour or beliefs offends us (or offends someone else, for example another client or potential client). The non-discrimination and cab-rank principles are important symbols of the core morality of our profession.

If the client insists, counsel should be prepared to argue any arguable case, even if it seems doomed to failure.

62 See *Arthur J S Hall & Co* v *Simons* [2002] 1 AC 615, 678, where Lord Steyn said that although the cab rank rule is "a valuable professional rule . . . its impact on the administration of justice in England is not great"; and Lord Hope added at p. 714 that although "[i]ts value as a rule of professional conduct should not be underestimated . . . its significance in daily practice is not great".

63 A rare exception is the case of barrister Mark Mullins – a member of the Lawyers' Christian Fellowship – who, in 2006, was reprimanded by the Bar Council, and ordered to pay £1,000 costs, for declining, on conscientious grounds, to represent an illegal immigrant who wished to rely on a same-sex relationship as a basis for staying in this country: *Daily Mail Online* 26 July 2006.

In September 2020, Mr Justice Turner began a judgment in the High Court in Liverpool rejecting a civil claim with these words: "Cheryl Pile brings this appeal to establish the liberty of inebriated English subjects to be allowed to lie undisturbed overnight in their own vomit-soaked clothing." Ms Pile had spent the night at a police station in Liverpool having been arrested for being drunk and disorderly. She claimed damages against the police for alleged assault because female officers had, for hygienic reasons, removed her outer clothing and provided her with a dry outfit to wear.[64]

Despite the lack of merit in his client's case, Ms Pile's counsel, Henry Gow, was right to argue it, if so instructed. Similarly in other hopeless cases, such as the 2015 claim by Jennifer Connell of Manhattan against her nephew, Sean Tarala, in the Connecticut Superior Court. He had greeted her exuberantly at his eighth birthday party, they fell over and she broke her wrist. William Beckert, her lawyer, argued that "a reasonable eight year old should have known that a forceful greeting . . . could cause the harms and losses suffered". Yes, this is what we sometimes do for a living. After forty minutes of deliberation, the jury dismissed the claim. It is only surprising that they took so long.[65]

[64] *Pile* v *Chief Constable of Merseyside Police* [2020] EWHC 2472 (QB).

[65] *The Times* 16 October 2015 and *National Law Journal* 19 October 2015. A very optimistic legal submission was made in 2013 by Romanian defence counsel for Radu Dogaru, who admitted stealing masterpieces by Picasso, Matisse and Gauguin from a museum in Rotterdam. Catalin Dancu, representing the defendant, said that Dogaru was considering suing the Dutch museum for "negligence with serious consequences" by

As Lord Hobhouse said in the Appellate Committee of the House of Lords in 2002, "it is the duty of the advocate to present his client's case even though he may think that it is hopeless and even though he may have advised his client that it is".[66] Lord Pearce put it more bluntly in the Appellate Committee in 1967: it is "easier, pleasanter and more advantageous professionally for barristers to advise, represent or defend those who are decent and reasonable and likely to succeed" in the litigation. But some clients are "unpleasant, unreasonable, disreputable and have an apparently hopeless case" and they too are entitled to have their case presented.[67]

Indeed, sometimes such people succeed in their claims or defences. Mr Justice Megarry observed in a 1970 judgment that, "As everybody who has anything to do with the law well knows, the path of the law is strewn with examples of open and shut cases which, somehow, were not; of unanswerable charges which, in the event, were completely answered; of inexplicable conduct which was fully explained".[68] In the Court of Appeal in 1963, Lord

failing to have an adequate security system to prevent the robbery: *International New York Times* 16–17 November 2013.

66 *Medcalf* v *Mardell* [2003] 1 AC 120, 143.

67 *Rondel* v *Worsley* [1969] 1 AC 191, 275. Cited with approval by Sir Thomas Bingham for the Court of Appeal in *Ridehalgh* v *Horsefield* [1994] Ch 205, 233. See also *Gallagher* v *Municipal Court of the City of Los Angeles* 192 P 2d 905, 908–909 (1948) (Supreme Court of California): "Even if a legal proposition is untenable, counsel may properly urge it in good faith; he may do so even though he may not expect to be successful, provided of course that he does not resort to deceit or to wilful obstruction of the orderly processes."

68 *John* v *Rees* [1970] Ch 345, 402 (Megarry J).

Justice Harman said that "if it be misconduct to take a bad point, a new peril is added to those of the legal profession".[69]

Like every advocate, I have argued quite a few arguable but hopeless cases for unpleasant clients, and indeed many hopeless cases for admirable people. Sir Thomas Bingham wisely stated in the Court of Appeal that "[i]t is rarely if ever safe for a court to assume that a hopeless case is being litigated on the advice of the lawyers involved".[70] Sometimes the client will only accept that she has no valid claim when the judgment of an independent court so states. And sometimes not even then. The duties of the advocate include advising the client, as objectively as possible, on the merits or otherwise of his case. If the claim or defence is unlikely to succeed – or doomed to failure – the client is entitled to know. But if the point is arguable, the client is entitled to say that he wishes to have it argued. I spend as much of my professional life advising people not to pursue hopeless cases as I do arguing hopeless cases. Like my advocacy in court, my advocacy in conferences with clients only sometimes succeeds.

69 *Abraham* v *Jutson* [1963] 1 WLR 658, 664. Lord Justice Harman added that it could only be misconduct if "a bad point is taken, knowing it to be bad and concealing from the court, for instance, an authority which shows it clearly to be a bad point". Lord Denning said at p. 663 that the advocate had taken bad points but the advocate "was not the judge of that. . . . An advocate is not to usurp the province of the judge. . . . He only becomes guilty of misconduct if he is dishonest, that is if he knowingly takes a bad point and thereby deceives the court".

70 *Ridehalgh* v *Horsefield* [1994] Ch 205, 234.

In such circumstances, the task of the advocate is to find the least hopeless point and focus on that. As the President of the Probate, Divorce and Admiralty Division, Sir James Hannen, said in a judgment in 1882, "[t]here is an honourable way of defending the worst of cases".[71] But there are limits: in 2019 the Pennsylvania Supreme Court suspended Thomas Peter Gannon, a lawyer in Delaware County, from practice for two years for "excessive and misplaced zeal" in that he filed at least forty-nine appeals in relation to a dispute about repairs to a client's property. The client had told Gannon to "shoot for the stars".[72]

If counsel is instructed to argue a weak claim, then, as Lord Justice Dyson said for the Court of Appeal in 2010, counsel "should not advance a submission but signal to the judge that he thinks that it is weak or hopeless by using the coded language, 'I am instructed that'".[73] Counsel should not echo the defence advocate in the *New Yorker* cartoon by Paul Noth in 2014: "In closing I would like to remind the jury that he says he didn't do it."[74] The defence advocate should certainly not tell the jury in his closing speech that he is doing his job "to [the] best of my ability with what I have had to work with", as occurred in a US District Court in 1968.[75]

So far I have been exploring counsel's duty to the client. But in assessing the ethics of advocacy, it is important

[71] *Smith* v *Smith* 7 PD 84, 89 (1882).

[72] *American Bar Association Journal*, posted 3 January 2019.

[73] *Richard Buxton* v *Mills-Owen* [2010] 1 WLR 1997, 2011.

[74] Paul Noth *The New Yorker*, 28 July 2014.

[75] *Matthews* v *US* 449 F 2d 985, 987n (US Court of Appeals, District of Columbia Circuit).

to emphasise that counsel also has duties to the court which can override her duties to her client.[76] As John Mortimer's barrister Rumpole put it, "I'm an old taxi, waiting on the rank, but I'm not prepared to be the get-away driver for a criminal conspiracy".[77] Henry Brougham, in his defence of Queen Caroline, wife of George IV, in 1820 against allegations of adultery, was wrong to say that the advocate has a "sacred duty" to "save" his client "by all expedient means – to protect that client at all hazards and costs to all others, and among others to himself".[78] Counsel should not adopt the approach taken by Jeffrey Lichtman, the New York attorney who represented "El Chapo", accused and convicted of running a vast drugs empire. Lichtman's description of the trial was that "we fought like complete savages and left it all on the battlefield . . . This was balls to the wall and that's how we fight cases".[79] Mr Lichtman's "savage" counsel is controlled, and rightly so, by a set of legal Queensberry rules which are designed to promote a fair

[76] *Bar Standards Board Code of Conduct*, Core Duty 1: "You must observe your duty to the court in the administration of justice". The guidance adds that this "overrides any other core duty". In *Giannerelli* v *Wraith* (1988) 165 CLR 543, 556, Chief Justice Mason said for the High Court of Australia that "[t]he duty to the court is paramount even if the client gives instructions to the contrary". This is the modern equivalent of the principle stated by Mr Justice Crampton in *R* v *Daniel O'Connell and others* (1844) 7 Ir LR 261, 312–313: the advocate has "duties as a man and as a Christian [which] are paramount to all other considerations".

[77] John Mortimer "Rumpole and the Bubble Reputation" in *The Best of Rumpole* (1993), p. 154.

[78] *Hansard*, House of Lords, 3 October 1820, column 114.

[79] *The Sunday Times* 17 February 2019.

hearing. As stated by section 188 of the Legal Services Act 2007, an advocate "has a duty to the court in question to act with independence in the interests of justice". This "overrides" any other obligation which the advocate may have – except "under the criminal law".

There are three specific duties owed by the advocate to the court which need to be emphasised. The first is that counsel must take all reasonable steps to ensure that the court has before it all relevant statutory provisions or rules and all relevant court decisions, including those unhelpful to his submissions.[80] I once succeeded in an asylum appeal in the Appellate Committee of the House of Lords on behalf of the Home Secretary because my opponent, Nicholas Blake QC (later a High Court judge), who was appearing for the asylum-seekers, found and disclosed a very persuasive judgment of the Canadian Federal Court of Appeal which supported my argument.[81]

However, the law reports contain many cases where counsel have failed, usually inadvertently, to draw the court's attention to relevant case-law or applicable statutory provisions. In 1921, Lord Birkenhead LC for the Appellate Committee of the House of Lords expressed disappointment

[80] *Bar Standards Board Code of Conduct*, Rule C3.4 and Guidance paragraph C5. See Brooke LJ in the Court of Appeal in *Copeland* v *Smith* [2000] 1 WLR 1371, 1375: "it is quite essential for advocates who hold themselves out as competent to practise in a particular field to bring and keep themselves up to date with recent authority in their field".

[81] *T* v *Secretary of State for the Home Department* [1996] AC 742. Lord Lloyd, for the Appellate Committee, said at p. 785 that it was the authority "from which I have derived the greatest help".

that counsel (including Sir John Simon KC) had failed to draw the attention of the Committee to a material section in the relevant statute. One of the Law Lords had discovered it after the case had been argued.[82]

The second important duty which counsel owes to the court is that "you must not abuse your role as an advocate",[83] for example by making statements or asking questions "merely to insult, humiliate or annoy a witness or any other person" (tempting though it sometimes is), or by making a serious allegation against any person unless you have reasonable grounds for doing so and the allegation is relevant to the case you are arguing, or by giving the court your personal view of the facts or law.[84]

The Bar Code of Conduct recognises an exception to not giving your personal views: that is where "you are invited

[82] *Glebe Sugar Refining Company Ltd* v *Trustees of the Port and Harbours of Greenock* (1921) WN 85. See also *Penrikyber Navigation Colliery Company Ltd* v *Edwards* [1933] AC 28, 33, where Viscount Dunedin said for the Appellate Committee of the House of Lords: "it is much to be regretted that neither the County Court judge nor the Court of Appeal had their attention directed by the Bar before them to . . . recent cases in this House . . . without a consideration of which it is impossible to determine the present question".

[83] *Bar Standards Board Code of Conduct*, Rule C3.2. Irving Kanarek acted as defence counsel for Charles Manson at his trial for the murder of Sharon Tate and others in 1970. As explained by the prosecutor in that trial, Vincent Bugliosi, in his book on the case, Kanarek "was something of a legend in the Los Angeles courts for his 'obstructionist tactics'". On one occasion, he "objected to a prosecution witness stating his own name because, having first heard his name from his mother, it was 'hearsay'": Vincent Bugliosi *Helter Skelter* (1992), pp. 378–379.

[84] *Bar Standards Board Code of Conduct*, Rules C3.2 and C7.

or required to do so by the court or by law".[85] I think if the judge or magistrate asks counsel's opinion, and there is no legal basis for her to do so, the advocate should decline (politely of course), reminding the tribunal that you are there to provide advocacy and not personal opinions. For counsel to give her views about the case would undermine the very essence of advocacy, that the barrister is speaking on behalf of the client. Indeed, for counsel to give a personal view would not assist the court when so many barristers have the capacity genuinely to believe that all of their clients have right (legal and moral) on their side.

Serjeant Buzfuz was therefore wrong in Charles Dickens' *Pickwick Papers* to tell the jury hearing the case of *Bardell* v *Pickwick* that he could only bear the responsibility of arguing such a matter because he is "buoyed up and sustained by a conviction so strong that it amounted to positive certainty that the cause of truth and justice or, in other words, the cause of his much-injured and most oppressed client, must prevail".[86] His personal opinions were irrelevant. In a 1957 episode of the television comedy *Hancock's Half Hour*, Tony Hancock, as the unsuccessful barrister, should not have told the jury that his client was such an honourable man that "I would be proud to call him my son".[87]

[85] *Bar Standards Board Code of Conduct*, Rule C7.4.

[86] (1837), chapter 34.

[87] *Hancock's Half Hour* broadcast on 2 December 1957, *The Crown* v *James (S)* (written by Alan Simpson and Ray Galton).

The abuse of the role of the advocate may take many forms. In 1879, the Court of Appeals of New York disbarred an attorney for the husband in divorce proceedings because he had spent a night in a hotel with the wife "for the purpose of procuring evidence" to be used in the proceedings.[88] Sir Thomas Bingham explained for the Court of Appeal in 1994 that it is "one thing for a legal representative to present, on instructions, a case which he regards as bound to fail; it is quite another to lend his assistance to proceedings which are an abuse of the process of the court".[89] An example of such an abuse is bringing proceedings which counsel knows have no legal basis and are being brought to embarrass or put pressure on the other party or a witness.[90] Nourse LJ said for the Court of Appeal in 1996 that "[t]he duty of counsel to put his client's case could not extend to advancing his client's belief, unsubstantiated by any evidence, that the judge was corrupt or biased. His duty in such circumstances was either to decline to comply with the instructions or to withdraw from the case".[91]

88 *In the Matter of William H Gale* 75 NY 526 (1879).

89 *Ridehalgh* v *Horsefield* [1994] Ch 205, 234.

90 See, for example, *R* v *Weisz ex parte Hector MacDonald Ltd* [1951] 2 KB 611 (Lord Goddard CJ for the Divisional Court). There is particular concern nowadays about the role of lawyers in what is known as "Lawfare" – that is the misuse of legal services and legal principles by very wealthy individuals and organisations that litigate with the object and effect of making the lives of their critics and opponents impossible. See the debate in the House of Commons on 22 January 2022, *Hansard*, column 565ff. Such conduct would be a breach of the duties of counsel not to abuse his powers.

91 *Thatcher* v *Douglas The Times* 8 January 1996.

Counsel enjoys a very wide latitude in what she says on behalf of her client in the courtroom.[92] But there are limits. Counsel cannot adopt what a trial judge described as "a form of courtroom anarchy". In 2013, in the Court of Appeal, Lord Judge, the Lord Chief Justice, reprimanded barrister Lawrence McNulty for his conduct of the defence of a man accused and convicted of terrorism offences. It was, said Lord Judge, "intolerable" that defence counsel had told the jury to ignore the trial judge, Mr Justice Henriques, "as a salesman of worthless goods" and (together with the prosecution counsel) "the agents of a repressive State".[93] For his conduct of the defence, Mr McNulty was found by the Bar Standards Board to have breached the rules of professional conduct and was suspended from practice for four months.[94]

The third important duty owed by counsel to the court is that "you must not knowingly or recklessly mislead

[92] In *Bagirov* v *Azerbaijan* (2020) 71 EHRR 30, paragraph 80, the European Court of Human Rights said that in deciding whether disbarment of an advocate for disciplinary reasons was proportionate, it was an "important consideration" that he was being punished for comments made in the courtroom and "the principle of fairness militates in favour of a free and even forceful exchange of arguments between parties" in that context.

[93] *R* v *Farooqi* [2014] 1 Cr App Rep 69 at paragraphs 73–74, 93(c), 115 (Lord Judge LCJ for the Court of Appeal).

[94] See Joshua Rozenberg *The Guardian* 31 July 2014 and William Clegg *Under the Wig: A Lawyer's Stories of Murder, Guilt and Innocence* (2018), pp. 197–199. Mr Clegg QC represented Mr McNulty at the disciplinary hearing. He commented in his book: "Personally, I am confident that if the only transgression had been referring to the judge as a second hand car salesman there would have been no formal complaint. The trouble was it was one of a number of transgressions."

or attempt to mislead the court".[95] Dr Johnson told Boswell that "[a] lawyer is not to tell what he knows to be a lie: he is not to produce what he knows to be a false deed".[96] This is an ancient principle of the advocate's profession. The Statute of Westminster 1275 said at chapter 29 that if any lawyer was responsible for "deceit of the court", he should be imprisoned for a year and barred from pleading again.[97] In a bizarre case in 2007, a barrister was jailed for twelve months after pleading guilty to perverting the course of justice by creating a fictitious legal precedent in a family law dispute.[98]

As the Supreme Court of Florida has explained, "the requirement to provide zealous representation, as contemplated under our ethical rules ... does not excuse engaging in misconduct, irrespective of one's intent to benefit the client". The court suspended from practice for three years a Miami criminal defence lawyer who had altered the photographs shown to a robbery victim during a deposition.[99]

[95] *Bar Standards Board Code of Conduct*, Rule C3.1.

[96] Samuel Johnson and James Boswell *The Journal of a Tour to the Hebrides*, 15 August 1773 (edited by Peter Levi, 1984), p. 169.

[97] Sir John Baker *An Introduction to English Legal History* (2019), p. 166. As there explained at p. 165, it was at the beginning of the thirteenth century that a body of professional advocates first appeared in England.

[98] *The Times* 20 September 2007. In 2022, a solicitor was struck off by the Solicitors Disciplinary Tribunal after admitting that he had failed to disclose the existence of a key piece of evidence because he feared that it would weaken his client's personal injury claim: *Law Society Gazette* 18 April 2022.

[99] *The Florida Bar* v *Jonathan Stephen Schwartz* (No. SC 17-1381, 17 February 2022, p. 15) and *American Bar Association Journal*, posted 23 February 2022.

The duty not to mislead the court may be breached in many different ways. In 1981, the Supreme Court of Florida ordered the suspension for thirty days of an attorney for appearing in court "on a stretcher attired in bedclothes", despite the fact that he was walking about in normal clothes the day before.[100]

The core of the duty not to mislead is that the barrister must not make submissions or ask questions which suggest facts that you know or are instructed are untrue or misleading.[101] There will be many occasions when counsel has good reason to *doubt* that the client is telling the truth. But there is an important difference between *suspecting* your

[100] *The Florida Bar* v *T David Burns* 392 So 2d 1325 (1981) (Supreme Court of Florida). In 2014, the Illinois Supreme Court suspended a lawyer, Michael Joseph Finn, for sixty days for faking an illness to avoid oral argument in a case before the 7th Circuit US Court of Appeals in Chicago. He had felt unprepared to present the case: *In Re Michael Joseph Finn* (Illinois Supreme Court, 14 March 2014). See *American Bar Association Journal*, posted 19 March 2014.

[101] *Bar Standards Board Code of Conduct*, Rule C6. See also *Re Robert A Branch* 449 P 2d 174, 181 (1969) (Supreme Court of California): "an attorney owes no duty to offer on his client's behalf testimony which is untrue. . . . An attorney who attempts to benefit his client through the use of perjured testimony may be subject to criminal prosecution . . . as well as severe disciplinary action". In *McKissick* v *US* 379 F 2d 754, 761 (1967), the US Court of Appeals, Fifth Circuit, said that if a defendant told his lawyer that he had committed perjury at his trial in denying the alleged offence, the lawyer had a "professional, ethical and public duty to report it" to the court, whether or not the defendant had authorised such action, and even if he had specifically instructed counsel not to make it known. That seems impossible to reconcile with the principle of legal professional privilege which guarantees the confidentiality of discussions about the case between the client and her lawyer.

client is guilty of the offence charged (or is otherwise telling lies), and a case where your client *tells* you that he committed the crime and still wants to plead not guilty.

If a mentally competent client admits to you that he committed the alleged crime, you cannot then suggest to prosecution witnesses that your client did not do so, you cannot call your client to give evidence to deny his guilt, you cannot present alibi evidence or call other witnesses to suggest that he is not guilty. But because the Crown must prove the criminal charge beyond a reasonable doubt, "there is no impropriety in seeking to show that the prosecution evidence has fallen short of proof".[102] You may question the reliability of the prosecution evidence by cross-examining the witness who claims to have seen the defendant burgle the house: how far away was she standing at the time, was it dark, was she wearing her glasses? You may make a closing submission to the jury that the prosecution has not produced evidence which makes them sure of your client's guilt.[103] As a Washington DC lawyer had engraved on pencils distributed by his firm in the 1990s, "Reasonable doubt at a reasonable price".[104]

102 Sir Malcolm Hilbery *Duty and Art in Advocacy* (1959), p. 10.

103 *Bar Standards Board Code of Conduct*, Guidance paragraphs C9 and C10. See the High Court of Australia in *Tuckiar* v *R* (1934) 52 CLR 335, 346 (1934): counsel had "a plain duty, both to his client and to the court, to press such rational considerations as the evidence fairly gave rise to . . . Whether he be in fact guilty or not, a prisoner is, in point of law, entitled to acquittal from any charge which the evidence fails to establish that he committed".

104 *New Yorker* 30 September 1996. In the television series *Boston Legal* (ABC, Series 4, Episode 11, 2007), Denny Crane, after securing a not guilty verdict from the jury for his client accused of murder, tells the

The scope of the advocate's duty not to mislead the court was considered by the Court of Appeal in 1996 in *Vernon* v *Bosley (No. 2)*.[105] The plaintiff had brought a personal injuries claim after two of his children were killed when travelling as passengers in a car driven by the defendant which went off the road and plunged into a river. The defendant admitted negligence. The plaintiff claimed damages for the psychiatric harm caused to him by watching unsuccessful attempts to save his children after the accident. At the trial of the damages claim, the plaintiff called evidence in support from a psychiatrist and from a psychologist. But, on his counsel's advice,[106] he did not disclose that a few weeks earlier, in family law proceedings, both those witnesses had given evidence that the plaintiff's condition had much improved.

Lord Justice Stuart-Smith for the Court of Appeal acknowledged that if the barrister knows that his client in a criminal case has previous convictions, but the court and the

press: "Reasonable doubt at a reasonable price." And see also Michael Connelly *The Night Fire* (2020), p. 144: after a spectacular courtroom success, counsel Mickey Haller tells the press "Reasonable doubt for a reasonable fee".

105 [1999] QB 18.

106 Counsel for the plaintiff relied on a distinction drawn by Lord Diplock in the Appellate Committee of the House of Lords in *Saif Ali* v *Sydney Mitchell & Co Ltd* [1980] AC 198, 220: "A barrister must not wilfully mislead the court as to the law nor may he actively mislead the court as to the facts; although, consistently with the rule that the prosecution must prove its case, he may passively stand by and watch the court being misled by reason of its failure to ascertain facts which are within the barrister's knowledge."

prosecution do not, then he is not under any obligation to disclose those convictions.[107] Similarly, in a civil case, counsel is not obliged to call witnesses who she knows would give evidence which would not be supportive of her client's case.

But, Lord Justice Stuart-Smith observed, it is different where there was a "failure . . . to correct an incorrect appreciation which the court will otherwise have as a result of [counsel's] conduct of this case hitherto". If, as in the *Vernon* case, "there is a danger that the court will be misled, it is the duty of counsel to advise his client that disclosure should be made". Counsel in the *Vernon* case was, he said, "walking a tightrope and . . . did not succeed in staying on it". Lord Justice Stuart-Smith concluded that if the client refuses to accept the advice to disclose the relevant material, counsel could no longer continue to act in the case.[108] Lord Justice Thorpe, otherwise agreeing, suggested that in such circumstances counsel had a duty to go further and disclose the material to opposing counsel. He also suggested a helpful principle for these difficult questions of professional ethics: "[t]here is a value in instinctive and intuitive judgment. . . .

107 However, counsel must not then suggest to the court that his client is of good character. See *Bar Standards Board Code of Conduct*, Guidance paragraph C12; but if mandatory sentences apply for persons with previous convictions, the advocate has a duty to assist the court to pass a lawful sentence and so must advise the client to consent to disclosure, and cease to act if the client refuses. Moreover, according to the Guidance, "if the court asks you a direct question you must not give an untruthful answer and therefore you would have to withdraw if, on your being asked such a question, your client still refuses to allow you to answer the question truthfully".

108 *Vernon* v *Bosley (No. 2)* at pp. 37–39.

The course that feels wrong is unlikely to be the safe course to follow".[109]

This dividing line between no duty to disclose damaging information but a duty to remove an incorrect impression caused by the way the case has been argued can, as Lord Justice Thorpe noted in the *Vernon* case, "give rise to finely balanced outcomes".[110] This can be seen from the contrasting results in two earlier cases.

In the first case, in 1951, there was a dispute about whether a contract had been entered into. The first witness called by the plaintiff was a Mr Meikle. When he began his evidence, counsel for the plaintiff asked him, "Do you live at 96 Church Road, Stoneygate, Leicester?" That leading question received the answer, "Yes". Counsel then established that Mr Meikle was a qualified engineer, he had served in the First World War and he was a prison governor for five years. What counsel did not disclose, though he knew the facts, was that Mr Meikle had been brought to court from prison where he was serving a sentence having been convicted of drunk driving. 96 Church Road was his permanent address, but not his current address.

After the defendant discovered these facts, the Court of Appeal dismissed his application for a new trial.[111] Lord

[109] *Vernon* v *Bosley (No. 2)* at p. 64. The third judge, Lord Justice Evans, dissented by reason of his analysis of the facts of the case: pp. 52–54. The Appellate Committee of the House of Lords dismissed an application for leave to appeal: p. 64.

[110] *Vernon* v *Bosley (No. 2)* at p. 62.

[111] *Tombling* v *Universal Bulb Company Limited* [1951] 2 TLR 289.

Justice Somervell accepted that "it would have been better if [counsel] had omitted to put the questions as to the witness's address and previous position as a prison governor", but he was satisfied that what happened was not a "trick".[112] Lord Justice Denning accepted that counsel "must not . . . knowingly mislead the Court, either on the facts or on the law". But he concluded that there was "nothing improper" in counsel's conduct of this case, although he said he would have taken a different view if the questions had been asked "knowingly to mislead the Court".[113]

The third judge, Lord Justice Singleton, dissented. Non-disclosure of convictions was one thing. But the question, "Do you live at 96 Church Road?" was inviting a positive and misleading answer. It was impossible to say whether the judge's knowledge of the true facts might have affected his assessment of the credibility of an important witness.[114]

I find much more convincing the dissenting judgment of Lord Justice Singleton that counsel had positively misled the court. More importantly, that was also the view of Lord Justice Thorpe in the *Vernon* case in 1996. For Lord Justice Denning to say that the leading question "Do you live at 96 Church Road?", as opposed to a neutral form of question such as "Where do you live?", was not intended to mislead is, as Lord Justice Thorpe said, "a charitable conclusion indeed".[115] I would add that whether the court was

[112] At p. 293. [113] At pp. 297–298. [114] At pp. 293–294.
[115] [1999] QB 18, 62–63.

misled seems to me to be an objective question not dependent on the intentions of counsel.

The contrasting case concerned a claim by a press photographer against a Chief Inspector of the Metropolitan Police for damages for alleged assault and false imprisonment. The dispute turned on rival versions of what had happened on 5 November 1958 in Trafalgar Square. Throughout the trial, the defendant police officer appeared in plain clothes and was referred to by his counsel as "Mr". The judge (in summing-up the case) and plaintiff's counsel (in putting questions in cross-examination) referred to him as "inspector" or "chief inspector". What was known to the defendant's counsel, but not to the plaintiff's counsel or to the judge, was that between Guy Fawkes Night and the trial of the civil claim, the defendant had been demoted from the rank of Chief Inspector because he had been party to an arrangement, in another case, to deceive a court as to which police officer had arrested another alleged offender.

The Court of Appeal ordered a new trial because the judge and jury had been misled about the status of the defendant and this may have made a difference to the jury's verdict for the defendant. Lord Justice Holroyd Pearce said that counsel's "duty to the court was here unwarrantably subordinated to the duty to the client".[116] Lord Justice Willmer added that "the course taken, which had the effect of deceiving the court, was taken deliberately. Counsel for the

[116] *Meek* v *Fleming* [1961] 2 QB 366, 379. The case was thereafter settled by the Metropolitan Police paying Mr Meek £2,000 in damages and all his costs: see *Hansard*, House of Commons, 9 March 1962, column 863.

defendant has so informed us with complete candour".[117] The defendant's leading counsel, Victor Durand QC, was suspended from practice for twelve months by a disciplinary tribunal presided over by Lord Chief Justice Parker.[118]

I have little doubt that a court today would agree that such conduct was a breach of the duty not to mislead the court. I also agree with the observation of Lord Justice Thorpe in *Vernon* that the strength of the advocate's duty is subject to "evolutionary change".[119] What may once have been acceptable would not be so today.

Even unintentionally to mislead the court can be very damaging to an advocate's prospects of persuading the court on behalf of his client, or indeed on behalf of clients in future cases. As Chief Judge Cardozo said for the Court of Appeals of New York in 1928, reputation at the Bar "is a plant of tender growth, and its bloom, once lost, is not easily restored".[120] A particularly egregious example of counsel who lost the ear of the court is Richard Liebowitz, a copyright lawyer who had misled the courts so often that in 2020 the US Court of Appeals, Second Circuit in New York upheld an order requiring him to notify the court's findings to that effect to all his clients and all courts hearing cases brought by him. He had, for example, been held in contempt "for repeatedly lying, including under oath, about the date his own

[117] At p. 382.

[118] *The Times* 12 January 1962 and 13 January 1962. His obituary stated that "many at the Bar felt he had been unfairly treated": *The Times* 13 October 1994.

[119] [1999] QB 18, 64.

[120] *People ex rel Karlin* v *Culkin* (1928) 162 NE 487, 492.

grandfather had died to justify his failure to attend a court conference".[121]

In assessing the ethics of advocacy, it is also important to bear in mind that there is a crucial distinction in principle, difficult though it may sometimes be to apply in practice, between impermissibly misleading the court and legitimately persuading it by skilful advocacy which deflects attention away from the strength of the case against your client. Chapter 29 of the Statute of Westminster 1275[122] did not recognise such a distinction. The penalty of imprisonment for a year, and the prohibition on future pleading, applied not only to the advocate who deceived the court but also to one who acted "to beguile the court" – or in the Norman French, "pur enginer la court".

This is much more restrictive than the traditional as well as the modern concept of advocacy. Cicero boasted that in his defence of Cluentius in 66BC, his speech was designed to "throw dust in the eyes of the jury".[123] In the Kander and Ebb musical *Chicago*, Billy Flynn, the sharp defence lawyer, sings that the way to impress the jury is to "give 'em an act with lots of flash in it, and the reaction will be passionate". As he explains, "How can they hear the truth above the roar?"

[121] *Usherson* v *Bandshell Artist Management* 19-CV-6368 (US District Judge Jesse M Furman, 26 June 2020), p. 2; upheld by the US Court of Appeals for the Second Circuit, 25 June 2021. See *American Bar Association Journal*, posted 29 June 2021.

[122] See n. 97 above.

[123] Quintilian *The Orator's Education*, Book 2, chapter 17.21 (edited and translated by Donald A Russell, 2001), p. 387.

and "How can they see with sequins in their eyes?"[124] It is one of the greatest songs ever written for lawyers, admittedly not a large category, especially since Miss Adelaide does not take up the offer when Nathan Detroit sings to her "Sue me" in *Guys and Dolls*, and the Sharks and the Jets are not prosecuted in *West Side Story*.

The advocate often needs to explain away the evidence or authorities against his client. There is substance in the suggestion made to Alan M. Dershowitz, the prominent US lawyer, by his son, a professional magician: "You and I both do the same thing ... sleight of hand – making things appear to be what they're not."[125] In a personal injuries case in Philadelphia in 2009, counsel for the plaintiff filed a motion asking the judge to prohibit defence counsel, Stephen G. Leventhal, from following his practice of performing magic tricks for the jury during his submissions and then suggesting to them that the evidence for the other side is not what it seems. The case was settled and so the judge did not need to rule on Mr Leventhal's argument that the court should make the plaintiff's motion disappear.[126]

Focusing the attention of the judge or jury away from the merits of the case is not a new feature of advocacy. Quintilian referred to a case where an advocate representing a young child lifted him up and displayed him close to the jury. "What am I to do?", lamented the opposing advocate to

[124] "Razzle Dazzle" in *Chicago* (1975) by John Kander and Fred Ebb.

[125] Alan M Dershowitz *Reversal of Fortune* (1991), p. 207.

[126] The case was *Blash* v *ABA Construction Group*. See *The Legal Intelligencer* (Philadelphia), 2 March 2019.

his client, a large adult. "I can't hump *you* around."[127] Quintilian also drew attention to how

> Antonius, defending Manius Aquilius, tore open his client's clothes and disclosed the scars he bore in front, earned in his country's service, and thus, instead of relying on his own eloquence, delivered a shock to the eyes of the people of Rome, who, we are led to believe, were chiefly moved to acquit him by the mere sight. . . . So also, it is thought, Phryne was saved from danger not by Hyperides' pleading, admirable as it was, but by the sight of her lovely body, which she had further revealed by opening her dress.[128]

There are many examples of lawyers attempting to distract judges and juries, some of the conduct less compliant with the ethics of advocacy than others. Travers Humphreys in his recollections of life at the bar at the end of the nineteenth and in the early twentieth century, described the performance of defence counsel, Thorne Cole, who was frequently briefed for alleged railway pickpockets. He would focus on the difficulty in identifying the culprit in the confusion of a crowded railway platform when the train was getting ready to depart. His advocacy included "stamping on the ground, knocking a book or two off the desk and imitating the waving of the green flag and the blowing of the whistle by the guard. . . . With a large book held in both hands he would bang repeatedly on the desk in front of him with, at first, intervals of a second or

[127] Quintilian *The Orator's Education*, Book 6, chapter 1 (edited and translated by Donald A Russell, 2001), p. 41.

[128] Quintilian *The Orator's Education*, Book 2, chapter 15 (edited and translated by Donald A Russell, 2001), pp. 353–354.

so, rapidly lessening as the train was supposed to be gathering speed, until any books or papers belonging to other counsel would be jumping about".[129]

At the beginning of the twentieth century. Sir Edward Marshall Hall would have his clerk arrange on his desk in court his pill box, medicines, a variety of coloured pencils, and "his nose-spray … which, according to his opponents, he would be certain to use in order to divert the attention of the jury when the case was going against him".[130] Clarence Darrow, the great American defence attorney in the early decades of the twentieth century, feigned indifference as the prosecution called its first witness. He "settled down in his chair and … took a leisurely crack at the crossword puzzle in

[129] Travers Humphreys *Criminal Days* (1946), p. 40. Note that one of John Stuart Mill's objections to advocacy (see n. 14 above) was that an "Old Bailey counsel" boasts about "the number of pickpockets whom, in the course of a long career, he had succeeded in rescuing from the arms of the law". Travers Humphreys also described at p. 98 the technique of another defence counsel, George Elliott. His only cross-examination had been of the surveyor who gave evidence about the plan of the Turkish bath where the defendant and others were arrested: "He got the admission that the room where the men were is approached by a swing door, and you cannot see through a swing door. No one has ever suggested that they did see anything through the swing door, but that doesn't matter to George. He is now addressing the jury on the assumption that the issue in the case centres round that swing door." When Elliott began "waving his hands and swaying his body to and fro, and some of the jury are beginning to do the same", it became clear that the jury would acquit his client.

[130] Edward Marjoribanks *The Life of Sir Edward Marshall Hall* (1929), p. 378. See also C P Harvey QC *The Advocate's Devil* (1958), p. 30.

his morning paper".[131] And an even more extreme example, during the judge's summing-up to the jury at the end of a criminal trial in Canada in the 1980s, the defence advocate tried to distract the jury from focusing on the evidence most damaging to his client by "brushing his teeth at the counsel table".[132]

The line between impermissibly misleading the court and trying legitimately to focus its attention away from the case against your client may sometimes be hard to define, but it does exist. If, as has been alleged,[133] one of the defence counsel in the O. J. Simpson trial – the defendant was accused of murdering his ex-wife and her friend – replaced a nude photograph of the defendant's girlfriend with a photograph of the defendant's elderly mother (fully clothed) on his bedside table when the judge and jury came to view the house, this was a clear case of misleading the court.

In 1982, the Supreme Court of Wyoming found in contempt of court an attorney acting for the plaintiff in a civil trial for his conduct during cross-examination of one of the defendants. Counsel had kicked the defendant so hard that he fell into the jury box. Counsel explained that he was seeking to reconstruct the incident which led to his client's injuries for

[131] Donald McRae *The Old Devil – Clarence Darrow: The World's Greatest Trial Lawyer* (2009), p. 274.

[132] Peter V MacDonald QC *Court Jesters* (1985), p. 29. See also the unprofessional conduct of the lawyer "Citizen N" (as the court documents called him), caught by a surveillance camera in southern Siberia in 2016 eating a document to destroy the evidence which proved that his client was guilty of drunk driving: *The Times* 28 April 2016.

[133] Dominick Dunne *Justice* (2001), p. 241.

which he was suing the defendant. The court said that it was not impressed by the argument that counsel "was simply discharging his obligation to represent his client zealously".[134] Even Henry Brougham[135] would have thought that was going too far.

Similarly unprofessional and impermissible – though very effective – were the tactics of the New York defence lawyer, William F. Howe, at the end of the nineteenth century. The wife and children of the defendant would be placed in the first row of the court to attract the sympathy of the jury for their husband and father. That is fine but, as described by Richard M. Revere in his

[134] *Horn* v *District Court, Ninth Judicial District* 647 P 2d 1368, 1372 (1982) (Supreme Court of Wyoming). In the Netflix series *Better Call Saul,* Series 5, Episode 4, the shady lawyer Saul Goodman was defending a man accused of robbery at a shop. The owner of the shop, the only prosecution witness, was asked whether he saw the culprit in court, and he pointed to the man sitting in the defendant's seat next to Goodman. He was cross-examined by Goodman: was it dark (no, there was good lighting), did he get only a fleeting glimpse of the robber (no, he had a good look at the defendant during the robbery and stared him in the face), could he be sure it was the defendant (yes, he was), surely he must have a little doubt (no, he was certain). Goodman turned to face the public gallery: "Will the defendant please stand." The defendant was at the back of the court, the man sitting next to Goodman being a stand-in who looked vaguely like the defendant. Very effective but in 1981 the US Court of Appeals held that it was a contempt of court for defence counsel to substitute another person for his client at counsel's table in court with intent to cause a misidentification: *US* v *Thoreen* 653 F 2d 1332 (1981) (US Court of Appeals, Ninth Circuit), cert denied 455 US 938 (1982).

[135] See n. 78 above.

compelling study of the law practice of Howe and his partner, "if by chance a particular defendant did not have a pretty wife, fond children, or a snowy-haired mother, he was not for that reason deprived of the sympathy they might create on his behalf. Howe would supply them from the firm's large stable of professional spectators. Repulsive and apelike killers often turned up in court with lamblike children and wives of fragile beauty".[136]

Socrates had higher standards, as he explained in his unsuccessful defence to the charges of not believing in the gods and corrupting the youth of Athens in 399 BC. He said he would not be producing his children in court "to excite as much pity as possible" from the jury. Such conduct, he told the court, "would be discreditable to myself, and to you, and to the whole state".[137]

Over-zealous advocacy may lead an appeal court to conclude that a jury has been "misled" by the speeches of counsel.[138] In 1901, the Court of Appeal allowed an appeal from a jury award of damages in a libel trial because the advocacy of the plaintiff's counsel, Sir Edward Marshall Hall, was responsible for "inflaming the damages ... out of all proportion to the circumstances of the case". Sir Edward had made what the Master of the Rolls, Sir Richard Henn Collins, described as "a monstrous charge" against the

[136] Richard H Rovere *Howe and Hummel* (1947), pp. 57–58.

[137] Plato "The Apology" in *Portrait of Socrates* (translated by Sir R W Livingstone, 1938), pp. 34–35.

[138] *Praed* v *Graham* (1889) 24 QBD 53, 55 (Lord Esher MR for the Court of Appeal).

defendant's advisers.[139] A modern example is the decision of the District Court of Appeal of the State of Florida in June 2021 to allow an appeal from a jury verdict of more than $27 million against two tobacco companies in favour of a man whose wife had died of lung cancer. Judge Jeffrey T. Kuntz concluded that the claimant's counsel had impermissibly "inflamed the jury" by comparing the companies to Big Brother, the totalitarian state in George Orwell's novel *1984*. In a separate opinion, Judge Robert M. Gross persuasively suggested that this was "hardly the type of argument that would inflame the jurors and cause them to abandon all reason in returning a verdict".[140]

[139] *Chattell* v *Daily Mail Publishing Company Limited* (1901) 18 TLR 165. For the background see Edward Marjoribanks *The Life of Sir Edward Marshall Hall* (1929), chapter VII.

[140] *RJ Reynolds Tobacco Company and Philip Morris USA Inc* v *Mahfuz* (No. 4D 19-2236, 30 June 2021) (District Court of Appeal, Fourth District, Florida). Judge Gross agreed with the decision to overturn the jury verdict but only because of earlier judgments of the court by which he considered himself bound. He cited the judgment of Judge Learned Hand in *United States* v *Garsson* 291 F 646, 649 (1923) in the US District Court, New York: "Juries are not leaves swayed by every breath." On the *Mahfuz* case see *American Bar Association Journal*, posted 8 July 2021. In a civil damages claim before a jury, counsel should not ask the members of the jury to put themselves in the shoes of the plaintiff when deciding how much to award. That is impermissibly to invite the jury "to depart from neutrality and to decide the case on the basis of personal interest and bias rather than on the evidence": *Spray-Rite Serv Corp* v *Monsanto Co* 684 F 2d 1226, 1246 (1982) (US Court of Appeal, 7th Circuit), affirmed on other grounds 465 US 752 (1984) (US Supreme Court). On counsel making literary allusions, see also Chapter 1 at nn. 110–112.

Some advocates have accompanied their submissions with tears. Clarence Darrow "could weep at will – real tears".[141] And in one case, Darrow's closing speech made the judge cry.[142] Sir Edward Marshall Hall "wept before the jury and allowed the tears to stream down his cheeks as he spoke".[143] In 1897, the Supreme Court of Tennessee, dismissing an appeal from a judgment for a plaintiff who claimed she had been seduced under a promise of marriage, rejected the contention that counsel for the plaintiff should not have shed tears at the trial. The court noted that some counsel "deal wholly in logic" while "others use rhetoric and occasional flights of fancy and imagination. Others employ only noise and gesticulation . . . Others appeal to the sympathies – it may be the passions and peculiarities – of the jurors". The court pronounced that for an advocate able to shed tears, this was "one of the natural rights of counsel which no court or constitution could take away". Indeed, the court added, bizarrely, that if counsel has tears at his command, "it may be seriously questioned whether it is not his professional duty to shed them whenever proper occasion arises".[144]

141 John Farrell *Clarence Darrow: Attorney for the Damned* (2011), p. 215. In his final speech on behalf of a defendant acquitted of murder at a trial in Texas in 1911, another counsel sang to the jury, through his tears, "Home sweet home": William Durran *The Lawyer: Our Old-Man-of-the-Sea* (1913), pp. 56 and 214.

142 Donald McRae *The Old Devil – Clarence Darrow: The World's Greatest Trial Lawyer* (2009), p. 292.

143 Lord Birkett *Six Great Advocates* (1961), p. 14.

144 *Ferguson* v *Moore* (1897) 39 SW 341, 343 (Supreme Court of Tennessee). Tears from a prosecutor may raise different issues: see nn. 151–153 below.

Clarence Darrow once ended his closing speech to the jury by reciting aloud the lyrics of "The Star-Spangled Banner" – though the jurors convicted his client.[145] William F. Howe "made an entire summation, hours long, on his knees".[146]

There is one category of counsel who most definitely should not be seeking to throw dust in the eyes of judge or jury. Prosecuting counsel in a criminal trial has a duty "to act as a Minister of Justice", fairly presenting the case for the Crown, a role which "excludes any notion of winning or losing".[147]

[145] John Farrell *Clarence Darrow: Attorney for the Damned* (2011), p. 314.

[146] Richard H Rovere *Howe and Hummel* (1947), p. 69. Similarly at p. 132.

[147] *Randall* v *The Queen* [2002] 1 WLR 2237, paragraph 10(1) (Lord Bingham for the Judicial Committee of the Privy Council) and *Benedetto* v *The Queen* [2003] 1 WLR 1545, paragraph 54 (Lord Hope for the Judicial Committee of the Privy Council). In 2014, the Court of Appeal criticised prosecution counsel, Timothy Raggatt QC, for "a lamentable failure of the prosecutor's obligations" by not disclosing the existence of material which undermined the prosecution case in a criminal trial: *Conrad Steven Jones* v *R* [2014] EWCA Crim 1337, paragraph 33. In *A Drink at the Bar* (2021), p. 123, Graham Boal quotes Sir John Nutting, a distinguished First Senior Treasury Counsel, as saying that "the Crown gains no victories nor suffers any defeats". In *Famous Trials 7* (1962), p. 242, H Montgomery Hyde said that Sir Edward Clarke, acting for Oscar Wilde, was very critical of the conduct of the prosecutor, Sir Frank Lockwood QC, after Wilde was convicted of criminal offences: Lockwood had forgotten that "he is not here to try to get a verdict by any means he may have, but that he is here to lay before the jury for their judgment the facts on which they will be asked to come to a very serious consideration". In *The Art of the Advocate* (revised edition, 1993), p. 132, Richard du Cann QC suggested that the duty of Crown counsel to try to "get as near to the truth as he can and not to secure a verdict" applies in civil as well as criminal cases.

The prosecutor may cross-examine robustly, and make a closing speech that pulls no punches, but must do so fairly. In 1998 the Judicial Committee of the Privy Council allowed an appeal from a conviction for murder in Trinidad and Tobago because the prosecutor made what Lord Steyn described as "a wholly improper speech" containing "emotional appeals for sympathy for the deceased and his family ... [and he] demanded that the jury should not let the defendant 'get away with it'".[148] Nowadays, in the Crown Court the more obviously unfair the prosecutor, the less likely she is to secure a conviction: juries recoil from unfairness.

A similar duty of fairness applies to prosecuting counsel in the USA. The Supreme Court stated in 1928 that he "may prosecute with earnestness and vigour – indeed he should do so. But, while he may strike hard blows, he is not at liberty to strike foul ones".[149] In practice, however, the

148 *Allie Mohammed* v *The State* [1999] 2 AC 111, 125. Racist remarks by the prosecutor led to the quashing of a conviction in *Re Nathan House* (1921) 16 Criminal Appeal Reports 49, 51–52 (Court of Criminal Appeal). The closing speech of the Attorney-General, Sir Edward Coke, prosecuting and securing the conviction of Sir Walter Raleigh on the charge of high treason in 1603, is an example of how not to prosecute: "thou are a monster". See also Arthur Koestler *Darkness at Noon* (translated by Philip Boehm, 2019), p. 254: the Public Prosecutor's speech ends, "I demand that dogs gone mad should be shot – every one of them".

149 *Berger* v *US* 295 US 78, 88 (1935) (Mr Justice Sutherland for the US Supreme Court). On "foul blows" see *The Independent* 14 December 1988, reporting that after his client was convicted in Sonora, California of breaking and entering, defence attorney Clark Head said that he would be appealing on the ground that during his closing speech to the jury the prosecutor "farted about 100 times". On the duty of a

position in the USA too often remains as described by H. L. Mencken in 1926: the prosecutor is allowed to display "an extravagance of attack that would land him in jail, and perhaps even in a lunatic asylum, in any other country".[150]

In 1957 the Supreme Court of Illinois overturned a conviction for murder in part because of the highly prejudicial conduct of the prosecutor – he wept during his closing speech to the jury and said "I am not ashamed of what I am doing now, believe me. I knew the dead man".[151] By contrast, the Supreme Court of Arizona dismissed an appeal against a conviction for murder after the prosecutor shed "spontaneous and uncontrollable" tears during the evidence of the victim's mother.[152] At the Old Bailey in 1997, prosecuting counsel broke down and required a ten-minute adjournment while

prosecutor in the USA, see also *Remus* v *US* 291 F 501, 511 (1923) (US Court of Appeals for the Sixth Circuit): "This court has never regarded with favour arguments by a district attorney calculated to inflame the minds of the jurors and prejudice them against the accused. On the other hand, the district attorney has the right, and it is no doubt his duty, so long as he confines his argument to the evidence in the case, to present the government's side of the case in forcible and direct language". In *State* v *Gunderson* 144 NW 659, 660 (1913), the Supreme Court of North Dakota allowed an appeal against conviction after the prosecutor told the jury "I do not come here to try a case unless the defendant is guilty".

150 H L Mencken *Notes on Democracy* (1926), p. 169, cited in Fred R Shapiro *The Oxford Dictionary of American Legal Quotations* (1993), p. 352.

151 *The People of the State of Illinois* v *Dukes* (1957) 146 NE 2d 14, 17. On tears in court by counsel other than the prosecutor, see nn. 141–144 above.

152 *State of Arizona* v *Bailey* (1982) 647 P 2d 170, 172 and 175.

describing the systematic torture of a baby before he was killed. The defendant, the boyfriend of the baby's mother, had admitted manslaughter.[153]

Legal culture differs depending on the jurisdiction. Prosecuting counsel in this country would not adopt the style of Alan Jackson, the Los Angeles deputy district attorney in the successful prosecution in 2009 of music producer Phil Spector for the murder of Lana Clarkson, a cocktail hostess and B-movie actress whom Spector shot dead after taking her back to his home. The prosecutor asked the jury to imagine the one thing they would say to Ms Clarkson before she climbed into Phil Spector's car on the night of her death. "You are all thinking the same thing", he suggested. "You'd say 'Lana, whatever you do, don't go'."[154]

Whatever the jurisdiction in which the issues arise, identifying the limits of ethical advocacy is a difficult task. It is problematic in part because it has been well understood since at least the time of Cicero's description of the role of the orator in 55 BC that some judges and juries "decide far more problems by hate, or love, or lust, or rage, or sorrow, or joy, or hope, or fear, or illusion, or some other inward emotion, than by reality, or authority, or any legal standard, or judicial precedent, or statute".[155] The advocate cannot be expected to ignore such considerations when seeking to perform the important function of putting the case as persuasively as

[153] *The Times* 2 October 1997. [154] *The Guardian* 13 April 2009.

[155] Cicero *On the Orator* (translated by E W Sutton and H Rackham, 1948), Book 2, chapter 42, p. 325, where Cicero is quoting the advocate Marcus Antonius.

possible for the client, whoever he is, and irrespective of what the advocate may think of the strength or otherwise of the legal or ethical position being advanced.

The choice of styles of advocacy will depend of course on the personality of the advocate, the nature of the case and the identity of the tribunal.[156] Tears from an advocate, the use of magic tricks, or submissions delivered on your knees are unlikely to assist in most courts.

[156] In the prorogation case, *R (Miller)* v *Prime Minister* [2020] AC 373, mindful that we needed to persuade the Supreme Court that the case concerned an issue of law, not politics, I adopted a very low-key approach for my client, Gina Miller. My colleague, Aidan O'Neill QC, representing Ms Joanna Cherry MP and other claimants, relied in his submissions on the Battle of Bannockburn, quoted Oliver Cromwell, Abraham Lincoln and Nelson Mandela, and described the Prime Minister as the "father of lies" seeking to close down the "mother of Parliaments". Those comments did not find their way into the law report summary of his legal argument at [2020] AC 373, 384–386.

3

The Future of Advocacy

In 1818, Lord Ellenborough, the Lord Chief Justice, and three other judges in the Court of King's Bench decided that trial by battle remained a part of English law.

Mary Ashford had been raped and murdered. Abraham Thornton had been tried and acquitted of the crimes. Mary's brother, William Ashford, sought to reopen the case against Thornton by use of an ancient "appeal of felony" procedure. Thornton responded that he was then entitled to trial by battle. Lord Ellenborough agreed: "it is our duty to pronounce the law as it is, and not as we may wish it to be".[1] But then Lord Ellenborough was, as Lord Simon said in his analysis of the case in an Appellate Committee judgment in 1972, "probably the most conservative judge ever to sit on the English bench".[2]

William Ashford decided not to risk trial by battle and so abandoned his case against Abraham Thornton. A year later, in 1819, Parliament abolished the "appeal of felony" procedure, and the consequent right to trial by battle.[3] This was regretted by Mr Justice Harman in 1954 when

[1] *Ashford* v *Thornton* (1818) 1 B & Ald 405, 460.

[2] *McKendrick* v *Sinclair* [1972] SLT 110, 117. Lord Simon also pointed out that the *Ashford* case was heard "at a time when the duel was far from discountenanced (a Foreign Secretary had recently fought one and a Prime Minister was shortly thereafter to do so)".

[3] 59 George III, Chapter 46.

hearing a dispute between one boxer and another as to which of them was entitled to be called the welterweight champion of Trinidad.[4] In 2020, David Ostrom, facing legal problems after his divorce, unsuccessfully asked a court in Kansas, USA to grant him the right to trial by combat with swords against either his ex-wife or her lawyer, citing *Ashford* v *Thornton*.[5]

There is, of course, no prospect of the legal system returning to physical force as the means of resolving legal disputes. But there is a real question whether courts will continue to hear competing oral arguments on each, or all, sides of the case, before judges and juries give their decisions. Advocacy faces three connected challenges: the demands of efficiency, the opportunities offered by technological innovation, and the risk that bright young lawyers will no longer wish to join and remain at the Bar.

First, efficiency. In 1869, the Appellate Committee of the House of Lords heard an appeal by William Sheddon and his daughter about whether Mr Sheddon was the legitimate

4 *Serville* v *Constance* [1954] 1 WLR 487, 491.

5 *The Times* 16 January 2020. In the US District Court in Oklahoma City in 1992, Judge Wayne E Alley said: "I suppose counsel have a penumbral constitutional right to regard each other as schmucks, but I know of no principle that justifies litigation pollution on account of their personal opinions". He added that their conduct "makes me lament the demise of duelling": *American Bar Association Journal*, November 1992, p. 44. Note also in this pugilistic context that in 1990, a Texas lawyer, Tom Alexander, representing one of the defendants in civil proceedings, allowed the plaintiff and her lawyers to hit him in place of a $50,000 settlement from his client. Mr Alexander explained that his client was "very pleased" as "[h]e likes to have a lawyer . . . who will go to the mat for him": *The Washington Post* 19 October 1989.

son of his parents. The law report records that when the case was called on for the hearing, counsel for the Appellants was "unprepared" and so "it became necessary" for Miss Sheddon to address the House – "which she did for twenty-three days". Her father then "spoke for two days". In dismissing the appeal, the Lord Chancellor, Lord Hatherley, understandably observed that "during the first three or four days of the discussion . . . all, I think, was said that fairly could be said upon the subject".[6]

An extreme case indeed. But when I joined the Bar in 1980, advocacy was still effectively unlimited in time. The case would last as long as it lasted. Judges would do little if any pre-reading of the documents.[7] There were

[6] *Shedden* v *Patrick and the Attorney General* LR 1 SC & Div 470, 474–475 (1869).

[7] A distinguished advocate of the late twentieth century, Mark Littman QC, recalled that in the Appellate Committee of the House of Lords, "Lord Reid, for example, normally preferred not to open his papers until he heard how the case was put by counsel orally. Other judges adopted the same attitude": Mark Littman QC in *The Judicial House of Lords 1876–2009* (edited by Louis Blom-Cooper, Brice Dickson and Gavin Drewry, 2009), pp. 425–426. See also Alan Paterson *The Law Lords* (1982), p. 36 and Alan Paterson *Final Judgment: The Last Law Lords and the Supreme Court* (2013), p. 73. In *MV Yorke Motors* v *Edwards* [1982] 1 WLR 444, 446, Lord Diplock stated for the Appellate Committee of the House of Lords that it was now "the uniform practice of *all* [his emphasis] members sitting on an appeal to have read in advance of the hearing the judgments below and [the] parties' written cases". Lord Diplock complained, at p. 447, that "detailed or elaborate" written cases did not assist the Appellate Committee ("The appellant's case runs to no less than 39 and a half single-spaced foolscap pages of detailed argument").

cases – I witnessed some of them – when one or more of the advocates had not done much more by way of preparation. Counsel would read out each paragraph of the pleadings, all the correspondence and lengthy extracts from the authorities. Some leading counsel would be appearing in more than one case at the same time. Their unfortunate juniors would be told to "keep the case going until I return".[8]

By the late 1980s and early 1990s, some senior judges decided that the system had to change. In 1989, Lord Donaldson, the Master of the Rolls, announced that the Court of Appeal would require skeleton written arguments "to reduce the amount of time spent in court whilst at the same time adhering to our long established tradition of oral argument in open court". He said that because of the cost of time in court, it was "vital that it is used economically and effectively". Lord Donaldson emphasised that this was not a first step towards "having very full arguments submitted in writing and then limiting oral argument in court to a very short period". He insisted that "the English Court of Appeal remains firmly wedded to its long established tradition of oral argument in open court".[9]

[8] See C P Harvey QC *The Advocate's Devil* (1958), p. 48: "When I came to the Bar it was very common for fashionable leaders to be engaged in several cases simultaneously and to move from court to court picking up first one and then another at whatever stage it might happen to have reached."

[9] *Practice Direction (Court of Appeal: Presentation of Argument)* [1989] 1 WLR 281. Sir John Donaldson MR had suggested in 1982 that counsel may wish to provide a skeleton argument in advance of the hearing but it was not compulsory at that time: *Practice Note – Court of Appeal: New*

In a case in the Appellate Committee of the House of Lords in 1990, Lord Templeman vented his frustration (as he often did), complaining about the "unlimited time" allowed in court for each litigant. The result, he said, was that courts were subjected to "torrents of words, written and oral, which are oppressive". He suggested that the remedy was for the judge to read in advance the pleadings, documents certified by counsel to be necessary, and short skeleton arguments, and then the judge would "limit ... the time and scope of oral argument".[10]

Advocacy was becoming subject to the requirements of efficiency; and all the better for it. Hearings are

Procedure [1982] 1 WLR 1312, 1315. He stated in 1983 that this innovation "has proved very successful": *Practice Note (Court of Appeal: Skeleton Arguments)* [1983] 1 WLR 1055. Some counsel had difficulty complying with the compulsory requirement after it came into force in June 1989. In May 1990, Lord Donaldson MR noted that "there is an unacceptably high incidence of failure to lodge skeleton arguments in time": *Practice Direction (Court of Appeal: Skeleton Argument Time Limits)* [1990] 1 WLR 794, 795. In 1987, the Commercial Court required counsel to submit written outlines of their submissions in advance of the hearing: *Practice Note* [1987] 3 All ER 799. On skeleton arguments, see also Michael J Beloff QC *Advocacy as Art* (Margaret Howard Memorial Lecture 2000), pp. 27–30.

10 *Banque Keyser Ullman SA* v *Skandia (UK) Insurance Co Ltd* [1991] 2 AC 249, 280–281. See also Lord Templeman's speech for the Appellate Committee in *JH Rayner (Mincing Lane) Limited* v *Department of Trade and Industry* [1990] 2 AC 418, 483: "Ten counsel addressed the appellate committee for 26 days. This vast amount of written and oral material tended to obscure [the] fundamental principles ... In my opinion the length of oral argument permitted in future appeals should be subject to prior limitation by the Appellate Committee." See also n. 15 below on the *JH Rayner* case.

now regulated by timetables agreed or imposed in advance. Judges read skeleton arguments, the main documents and authorities in advance of the hearing, which can then focus on the core issues in dispute. When witnesses give evidence, judges prevent repetitive cross-examination.[11] Advocacy is shorter in length, and more intense in its focus – and indeed more intense in its demands on the advocate.

The impact of these reforms can be seen, for example, in the reduction in the length of hearings in the Appellate Committee of the House of Lords. In the period 1952–1968, 25 per cent of English civil appeals in the Appellate Committee occupied five days or more of court time, and 10 per cent of English civil appeals lasted seven days or more.[12] In the 1970s and early 1980s, a case in the Appellate Committee of the House of Lords took four days on average.[13] In 2019–2021, cases in the Supreme Court (the successor to the Appellate Committee) lasted, on average, less than a day and a half and no case has occupied more than four days of court time, with the exception of a tax case which involved three appeals to the Supreme Court (as well as three

[11] See, for example, *R* v *B* [2006] Crim LR 54, where the Court of Appeal (Criminal Division) said that in criminal trials judges were entitled to impose time limits on cross-examination to prevent counsel indulging in lengthy and repetitious questioning of a witness.

[12] Louis Blom-Cooper and Gavin Drewry *Final Appeal: A Study of the House of Lords in Its Judicial Capacity* (1972), pp. 234–235.

[13] Alan Paterson *Final Judgment: The Last Law Lords and the Supreme Court* (2013), p. 81.

references to the Court of Justice of the EU).[14] It is inconceivable that the Supreme Court today would sit for twenty-six days to hear one case, as the Appellate Committee did in 1989. Lord Templeman's speech for the Appellate Committee began: "these appeals raise a short question of construction of the plain words of a statutory instrument".[15]

The changes to court practice recognise that court hearings, civil or criminal, are expensive – for the litigants in a civil case, for the defendant in the criminal case who is paying or contributing to the costs of a defence, and for the state, both in funding legal aid and in paying for the capital and running costs of the courtrooms and those who work in them.

In many other jurisdictions, oral advocacy is much more confined in its length. In the early days of the United States Supreme Court, at the beginning of the nineteenth century, lawyers such as Daniel Webster would deliver their arguments without limitation of time, and without interruption by the Justices. Cases could last as long as ten days. The Justices would leave the bench while argument continued in

[14] *Test Claimants in the FII Group Litigation* v *Revenue and Customs Commissioners* [2021] 1 WLR 4354, paragraphs 1 and 21 (Lord Reed and Lord Hodge for the Supreme Court). The three appeals occupied one, three and four days of court time respectively. The information about the length of time taken by recent Supreme Court cases comes from the Supreme Court website, which lists judgments and identifies the number of days taken in oral argument. A case occupied eight days of Supreme Court time in 2011: *Durham* v *BAI (Run Off) Ltd (in scheme of arrangement)* [2012] 1 WLR 867.

[15] *JH Rayner (Mincing Lane) Limited* v *Department of Trade and Industry* [1990] 2 AC 418, 476. See also at n. 10 above for Lord Templeman's comments on the length of the oral argument in that case.

order to eat and drink.[16] Today, counsel arguing a case in the United States Supreme Court are allowed no more than thirty minutes on each side (with rare exceptions).[17] Much of that time is occupied by the Justices asking questions or giving answers of their own.

Chief Justice Hughes (who presided from 1930 to 1941) was especially strict in enforcing time limits. He is said on one occasion to have "called time on a leader of the New York Bar in the middle of the word 'if'". In another case, on being asked by the advocate how much time remained for his argument, the Chief Justice replied "14 seconds".[18]

Oral argument in federal courts of appeal in the USA, and in Canadian appeal courts, are also subject to time limits of an hour or less for each side. Civil law jurisdictions impose severe limits on oral advocacy. That influenced the practice in courts with a Europe-wide jurisdiction. The European Court of Human Rights disposes of over 99 per cent of applications without a hearing. When a hearing does take place, there is a thirty-minute limit for each side's oral submissions. The Court of Justice of the European Communities imposes

[16] Stephen M Shapiro *Oral Argument in the Supreme Court: The Felt Necessities of the Time* (1985 Address before the Supreme Court Historical Society) (available on the Mayer Brown website), pp. 2 and 5.

[17] In 1849 the court had ordered that no counsel should be permitted to speak for more than two hours without special leave. Further restrictions were later imposed. The time allowed was reduced to thirty minutes in 1970. See Stephen M Shapiro *Oral Argument in the Supreme Court: The Felt Necessities of the Time* (1985 Address before the Supreme Court Historical Society) (available on the Mayer Brown website), pp. 4–6.

[18] Edwin McElwain "The Business of the Supreme Court as Conducted by Chief Justice Hughes", 63 *Harvard Law Review* 5, 17 (1949).

similar time limits. Indeed (pre-Brexit), I – and many other counsel from the United Kingdom – would arrive at the court in Luxembourg for a hearing, having prepared a thirty-minute speech and distributed it to the interpreters, often then to be told by the President of the Court at the quaint behind-the-scenes meeting of judges and counsel immediately before the start of the proceedings, "we have a busy day today, so please limit your pleading to twenty minutes".

In recent years, there have been restrictions in the courts of the United Kingdom on the right to an oral hearing. Since 2016 there is no longer such a right on an application for permission to appeal to the Court of Appeal. The restriction was unsuccessfully challenged in the Court of Appeal, which held that it was necessary to strike a balance between the right to an oral hearing and the need to reduce delays in the hearing of substantive cases in that court. The balance struck was a fair one, said the Court of Appeal, given that the litigant seeking permission to appeal had already enjoyed a full hearing at first instance, and a decision by the trial judge and by a Court of Appeal judge on paper to refuse permission to appeal.[19] For similar reasons, it is only in very exceptional circumstances that the Supreme Court, by contrast with its predecessor the Appellate Committee of the House of Lords, holds an oral hearing of an application for permission to appeal.[20]

[19] *R (Siddiqui)* v *Lord Chancellor* [2019] EWCA Civ 1040 (Sir Timothy Lloyd). A very similar challenge also failed in the Inner House of the Court of Session in Scotland: *Prior* v *The Scottish Ministers* [2020] CSIH 36.

[20] The European Court of Human Rights has recognised that Article 6 of the European Convention on Human Rights (the right to a fair hearing)

In his 2016 review of the structure of civil courts, Sir Michael Briggs (since appointed to the Supreme Court as Lord Briggs) explained that no steps had been taken to reduce the length of oral hearings of full appeals in the Court of Appeal "because it is generally considered that this feature of the court's procedure is one of the jewels in its crown by comparison, for example, with the procedure of the Supreme Court of the USA, the European Court of Human Rights and the Court of Justice of the European Union".[21]

So United Kingdom courts continue to determine substantive civil and criminal cases, whether at first instance or on appeal, after hearing detailed oral submissions from the advocates, albeit in a manner much more efficient than in previous decades. Judges are now rightly concerned to impose timetables that ensure there is sufficient opportunity for counsel to present their arguments, and test the opposing case, but time is not wasted. There is recognition by judges – as well as lawyers – that to confine oral advocacy in appellate courts to thirty minutes for each side would impede the quality of

does not mean there must always be an oral hearing at the appellate level. Unsurprisingly, as that court disposes of 99 per cent of applications without an oral hearing. See *Miller* v *Sweden* (2006) 42 EHRR 1155, paragraph 30: the central question, after a hearing at first instance, is whether the appeal "raise[s] any questions of fact or questions of law which cannot be adequately resolved on the basis of the case-file".

[21] Lord Justice Briggs *Civil Courts Structure Review: Final Report* (July 2016), paragraphs 5.9, 9.5 and 9.8. He said that the removal of a right to an oral hearing on an application to the Court of Appeal for permission to appeal was "in order to preserve by the only means perceived to be available the larger prize of retaining the full oral presentation and argument of appeals for which permission is given".

justice, and impede the client's understandable wish to see that her arguments have been understood and addressed.

The question, to which I now turn, is whether technological developments will lead to substantial changes to this practice.

In the 1993 edition of his book *The Art of the Advocate*, Richard du Cann QC said that counsel argue cases "in a manner which has not changed basically for 200 years".[22] Of course, while the advocate's central function of appearing in court and presenting the client's case has not much altered, the advocate, like everyone else, has been affected by technological innovation. Since I began practice in 1980, the hand-written engagement diaries and accounts ledgers have disappeared from chambers. Case law, statutes and other materials are now accessed online. Documents are searched electronically for relevant information. Witnesses may give evidence from abroad by video link. Many counsel (I am not amongst them[23]) use electronic bundles of documents in court.

The Covid-19 pandemic made it necessary for advocates to make their submissions in virtual hearings, for which the Coronavirus Act 2020 made provision.[24] Most advocates mastered, or at least came to terms with, the previously unknown mysteries of Zoom, Microsoft Teams and other platforms. We learned that if you are representing a client

[22] Revised edition, 1993, p. 2.

[23] Philip Roth "went on using WordPerfect 5.1 (from 1989) until the bitter end": Blake Bailey *Philip Roth: The Biography* (2021), p. 751. And me.

[24] See sections 53–57 and Schedules 23–27.

during a remote hearing, it is wise to avoid following the example of the lawyer criticised by Judge Dennis Bailey in Broward County, Florida for appearing on screen "still in bed, still under the covers".[25] Peruvian lawyer Hector Robles did not realise his camera was on during a remote court hearing on Zoom while he was having sex with a woman said to be his client.[26] And who could forget seeing the video of Texas lawyer, Rod Ponton, confirming to Judge Roy Ferguson, "I am not a cat", after speaking during a court hearing in feline form because of a filter that he was unable to turn off.[27]

The pandemic required lawyers and judges to avoid such perils and to adapt to novel means of performing their

[25] *Miami Herald* 13 April 2020 and *The Times* 16 April 2020. Another Florida counsel appeared at a remote hearing without a shirt, and other advocates in United States courts fell asleep during such hearings or were seen smoking a cigar or drinking a glass of wine: *Louisville Courier Journal* 18 December 2020 and *American Bar Association Journal*, posted 16 February 2021. A lawyer was fined US$300 by the Michigan Court of Appeals for raising his middle finger at the court during a Zoom hearing. James Heos claimed that he had so signalled in frustration at a malfunctioning computer screen and not at the court, and he had no idea he could be seen: *Detroit Free Press* 28 May 2021 and *American Bar Association Journal*, posted 1 June 2021.

[26] Judge Torres suspended the hearing and issued a statement "condemning" Robles for committing "obscene acts which violated public decency": *The Times* 2 February 2021 and *Mail Online* 30 January 2021.

[27] *Daily Mail* 11 February 2021. Another Florida advocate, Samuel J Rabin Jr, wanted to attend a physical hearing to represent his client for sentencing after a criminal conviction but, anxious about Covid-19, he wore a full, disposable hazmat suit in court: *American Bar Association Journal*, posted 7 July 2020; and *National Law Journal* 6 July 2020.

existing functions. The judiciary, the court staff and the legal profession responded speedily and effectively to the challenges to keep the civil justice system functioning.[28] This was a remarkable achievement as courts were reliant on IT systems which the Lord Chief Justice, Lord Burnett, described in May 2020, with judicious understatement, as "rather antiquated".[29] The criminal courts found it more difficult to process cases during a pandemic, not least because jury trial depends on personal communication between members of the jury, and by them with the judge, which it would be impossible to replicate through a computer screen, and so cases could not be heard by Zoom.[30]

[28] See Richard Susskind *Online Courts and the Future of Justice* (updated paperback edition, 2021), p. xxv: "Policymakers and judges recognised that if court services were to be maintained, there was no choice but to embrace technology." He concluded, at p. xxxv, that "the UK Supreme Court responded more emphatically and successfully than any of its equivalents internationally".

[29] *Covid-19 and the Courts*, Report of the Constitution Committee of the House of Lords (HL Paper 257, 30 March 2021), paragraphs 37 and 40; and the Evidence of the Lord Chief Justice to the Constitution Committee, 13 May 2020, Q1. I declare an interest as a member of the Constitution Committee of the House of Lords which produced this report.

[30] Richard Susskind *Online Courts and the Future of Justice* (updated paperback edition, 2021), pp. xxvi–xxxvii. Section 198 of the Police, Crime, Sentencing and Courts Act 2022 introduced a new section 51 of the Criminal Justice Act 2003 conferring a power on the judge to allow the jury (all of the members together) to hear a criminal trial remotely from the judge, the witnesses and the lawyers. For the difficulties this would pose, see *Hansard*, House of Lords, 10 January 2022, columns 918–930.

Lord Burnett added that he was "confident" that after "engaging in the biggest pilot project that the justice system has ever seen", there will be "no going back to February 2020" in relation to how the courts use technology.[31] The then Lord Chancellor, Robert Buckland, agreed in July 2020 that "[r]eturning to the status quo would be a massively missed opportunity here".[32]

In May 2021, the Bar Council of England and Wales, the Bar Council of Northern Ireland, the Faculty of Advocates of Scotland and the Bar of Ireland published a statement accepting that the use of remote hearings should continue, post-Covid-19, to deal with "short or uncontroversial procedural business".[33] That must be right. For a preliminary or case management hearing, the giving of directions, extensions of time, or for the delivery of a judgment, the judge, counsel and the parties do not need to travel to a court building for a thirty-minute appointment that can be as effectively conducted on Microsoft Teams. But as the House of Lords Constitution Committee advised in March 2021, to take advantage of the potential for saving time and money by such

[31] *Covid-19 and the Courts*, Report of the Constitution Committee of the House of Lords (HL Paper 257, 30 March 2021), paragraph 288; and the Evidence of the Lord Chief Justice to the Constitution Committee, 13 May 2020, Q6.

[32] *Covid-19 and the Courts*, Report of the Constitution Committee of the House of Lords (HL Paper 257, 30 March 2021), paragraph 288; and the Evidence of the Lord Chancellor to the Constitution Committee, 22 July 2020, Q135.

[33] "Four Bars statement on the administration of justice post-pandemic", *The Bar Council*, 5 May 2021.

reforms, courts and tribunals need to be given adequate funding for improved technology.[34]

However, the Bars of the United Kingdom and Ireland did not think that remote hearings were acceptable for substantive trials, civil or criminal. The experience of counsel, they reported, was that virtual hearings were less effective than physical court hearings in identifying the issues and allowing effective argument because of the greater spontaneity of human interaction which being present together in a courtroom allows. "The universal sentiment across the four Bars", they stated, "is that remote hearings deliver a markedly inferior experience" for all concerned, and in particular the interests of the client. As pointed out by Guy Pratte, a distinguished Canadian advocate, a FaceTime dinner with friends is better than not seeing them, but it is markedly inferior to meeting in person – and the same is true of advocacy in a remote courtroom.[35] To echo a song from the musical *Hamilton*, counsel and client need to be in the room where it happens.

Remote hearings during the pandemic faced other difficulties: many litigants did not have the computer facilities or bandwidth or quiet home conditions or confidence to enable them to access virtual proceedings (although for some disabled people, a remote hearing was much less problematic than travelling to a physical courtroom); clients could not

[34] *Covid-19 and the Courts*, Report of the Constitution Committee of the House of Lords (HL Paper 257, 30 March 2021), paragraphs 62–64 and 297–298.

[35] Guy J Pratte, Foreword to the Report of the Advocates' Society, *The Right to Be Heard: The Future of Advocacy in Canada* (June 2021), p. 4.

easily communicate with their legal advisers during remote hearings; counsel could not so easily communicate with each other and so opportunities were lost to resolve issues by a quiet word along the advocates' bench; the press had difficulties obtaining information from some courts about which cases were being heard and when, and in any event virtual attendance deprived the press of the ability to check facts and learn about the background of the case by discussions with lawyers and others.[36] Looking at a screen is also much more tiring and requires more frequent breaks for judges and counsel.

All of these are factors to be taken into account when deciding how the legal system should amend traditional practices to use the possibility of remote hearings. The more fundamental question is whether advances in technology should encourage the legal system to remove the right of the client to oral advocacy by their lawyer, other than in exceptional cases.

The best informed and most persuasive analyst of the opportunities presented for the work of courts by modern technology is Professor Richard Susskind. He has been thinking, speaking and writing about the subject for nearly forty years. For much of that time he was, in the words of Lord Briggs, a "voice crying in the IT wilderness".[37]

[36] *Covid-19 and the Courts*, Report of the Constitution Committee of the House of Lords (HL Paper 257, 30 March 2021), paragraphs 41, 47–48, 51, 97–98, 104, 120, 123–124, 141–142.

[37] Lord Justice Briggs *The Online Solutions Court: Affordable Dispute Resolution for All* (Tom Sargant Memorial Lecture, Justice, 18 October 2016), paragraph 4.

He has been Technology Adviser to several successive Lord Chief Justices. He has found that amongst the professions, lawyers are the second most cautious about technological change, behind "only the clergy".[38] He reminds lawyers that his predictions in the 1990s that email would become the standard means of communication with clients and that the primary research tool would be the internet were ridiculed.[39] He predicts more substantial change in the near future.

Professor Susskind starts from the premise, and who could disagree, that resolving disputes through court hearings costs too much money, takes too much time and remains unintelligible to most people. We have a world-class legal system, with independent and expert judges, but the expense combined with the reduction in the scope and amount of legal aid[40] mean that fewer and fewer people can afford to access the facilities. When they do, they find

[38] Richard Susskind *Online Courts and the Future of Justice* (2019), p. 4. Though in the 2021 updated paperback edition at pp. xxviii–xxix, he recognised that "[t]he conventional wisdom . . . that the legal profession is deeply conservative and almost incapable of change" is rebutted by its response to the Covid-19 crisis as "judges and lawyers have rapidly put in place a rich new set of rules, procedures, protocols, and practice directions to enable court service to continue".

[39] Richard Susskind *Online Courts and the Future of Justice* (2019), pp. 2–3.

[40] From 2010/11 to 2015/16, annual legal aid spending fell at a rate of around 10 per cent per year. By 2019/20, expenditure on legal aid was 37 per cent less in real terms than it had been in 2010/11. See *Covid-19 and the Courts*, Report of the Constitution Committee of the House of Lords (HL Paper 257, 30 March 2021), paragraph 16.

that many of our court buildings are in a run-down state of disrepair.[41]

Professor Susskind argues that in order to promote access to justice we should do more than simply graft new technology onto existing methods for resolving disputes so they are refined and improved.[42] In his opinion, "[w]e are just warming up".[43] Access to justice requires, he says, a transformation of existing procedures. Like online banking, online judging will and should change the way in which business is conducted. It will involve judges receiving arguments and evidence in electronic form and delivering decisions electronically, "with no oral hearings, either in physical courtrooms or by video".[44]

This should begin, says Professor Susskind, with low-value civil disputes, but would then be extended to higher value litigation. By civil disputes, Professor Susskind

[41] See the comments of the Lord Chief Justice, Lord Burnett, *The Law Society Gazette*, 15 November 2018. And see Richard Susskind *Online Courts and the Future of Justice* (2019), pp. 27–28.

[42] Richard Susskind *Online Courts and the Future of Justice* (updated paperback edition, 2021), p. xxvii: "Almost all the remote courts that have been set up in response to the virus are variations on the theme of traditional courts. But we should be clear: dropping our current court system into Zoom is not, as some commentators like to intone, a 'shift in paradigm'."

[43] Richard Susskind *Online Courts and the Future of Justice* (updated paperback edition, 2021), p. xxxix.

[44] Richard Susskind *Online Courts and the Future of Justice* (updated paperback edition, 2021), pp. xxxix–xl. Online courts will, in his vision, also involve courts providing a service designed to encourage and support parties to resolve their disputes: pp. xl–xlii.

means non-payment of debts and other breach of contract disputes, personal injury and other negligence claims, and complaints about the dismissal of an employee. He has not specifically analysed family law, administrative law and criminal law. But he believes that much of his analysis applies to those areas too, while acknowledging that "criminality and its handling by court systems does raise some additional and difficult questions",[45] particularly in relation to jury trial.[46]

Professor Susskind recognises that in the online court, evidence and argument would still be submitted to the human judge, "for the first generation at least". But the methods by which the judge is assisted to reach her decision would be "transformed, with oral advocacy or lawyers in a courtroom *eliminated* [Professor Susskind's emphasis] from the process". For Professor Susskind, this involves no loss to society. And that is because, in his view, lawyers need to understand that "people do not really want you. They want the outcomes you bring". And, he believes, those outcomes – greater access to courts, with disputes decided or resolved more speedily, and at less cost, and in a manner which is comprehensible to the parties – do not require oral advocacy and may indeed be impeded by oral advocacy.[47]

[45] Richard Susskind *Online Courts and the Future of Justice* (2019), pp. 6–12 and 34.

[46] Richard Susskind *Online Courts and the Future of Justice* (updated paperback edition, 2021), pp. xxxv–xxxviii. See n. 30 above.

[47] Richard Susskind *Online Courts and the Future of Justice* (2019), pp. 50–52.

Professor Susskind's work greatly influenced Lord Briggs' review of the structure of the civil courts.[48] Lord Briggs recommended an online court in which the judge would determine disputes in claims up to £25,000 (excluding personal injuries and some other categories of case) without the need for participation by lawyers.[49] Lord Briggs rejected the complaint that this would be "second class justice". Guidance would help parties to present their claims and defences online, cases requiring hearings – whether face-to-face or virtual – would be identified and addressed accordingly, there would be the opportunity to seek to appeal against adverse decisions, and in any event a comparison with traditional litigation is unhelpful because "such litigation is so expensive that it is either unaffordable or imprudent, where modest sums are at stake, save where Legal Aid or some special costs regime (such as protects personal injury claimants)" is available.[50]

[48] Lord Briggs found that "the single, most pervasive and indeed shocking weakness of our civil courts is that they fail to provide reasonable access to justice for the ordinary individuals or small businesses with small or moderate value claims", with some exceptions. He explained that he had asked those attending consultation meetings, including legal professionals, "whether any of them would recommend to a non-legally qualified friend of theirs the undertaking of civil litigation (other than in relation to personal injuries) [where special costs provisions apply] in connection with a dispute with a value at risk of £25,000 or less". Lord Briggs said he could not recall a single occasion when any of the 1,000 consultees answered in the affirmative. See Lord Justice Briggs *Civil Courts Structure Review: Final Report* (July 2016), paragraph 5.15.

[49] Lord Justice Briggs *Civil Courts Structure Review: Final Report* (July 2016), paragraph 6.54.

[50] Lord Justice Briggs *Civil Courts Structure Review: Final Report* (July 2016), paragraphs 6.9–6.10.

Lord Briggs explained that it was "not a design objective of the Online Court to exclude lawyers". Parties could use lawyers if they wished. The "underlying rationale" was that, unlike the traditional courts, which are "only truly accessible by, and intelligible to, lawyers", the new online court should as far as possible be "equally accessible to both lawyers and litigants in person".[51] Use of the online process would be mandatory but "[m]any cases which cannot be settled will still be directed to a face to face trial", or a video hearing, depending on the circumstances, and "[s]everal types of case, where face to face determination is regarded as necessary, will be excluded from the Online Court altogether", such as claims for possession of homes.[52] He also proposed the exclusion, at least in the first instance, of non-monetary claims for an injunction or for specific performance because they "commonly raise issues of a complexity" which the first-generation online court could not address,[53] personal injury claims, class claims (including bankruptcy or winding up), and claims by or against minor children or other protected parties.[54]

Lord Briggs added that the online court project which he was proposing, with its "radically new and different

[51] Lord Justice Briggs *Civil Courts Structure Review: Final Report* (July 2016), paragraph 6.22.

[52] Lord Justice Briggs *Civil Courts Structure Review: Final Report* (July 2016), paragraph 6.79.

[53] Lord Justice Briggs *Civil Courts Structure Review: Final Report* (July 2016), paragraph 6.94.

[54] Lord Justice Briggs *Civil Courts Structure Review: Interim Report* (December 2015), paragraphs 6.43–6.49, with which the Final Report is to be read, as it states at paragraph 1.4.

procedural and cultural approach to the resolution of civil disputes", might, if successful, "pave the way for fundamental changes in the conduct of civil litigation over much wider ground" than the first stage, that is for money claims up to £25,000, with substantial exclusions.[55]

In September 2016, the Ministry of Justice and Her Majesty's Courts and Tribunals Service issued a joint "vision statement" which set out the government's plans for reform of the courts and tribunals, including proposals to make greater use of online proceedings.[56]

In 2017, the government published the Prisons and Courts Bill, which contained provisions to establish an online court procedure. The Bill fell when the Prime Minister, Theresa May, called the 2017 General Election. The relevant provisions were reintroduced in the Courts and Tribunals (Online Procedure) Bill in May 2019. That Bill completed its passage through the House of Lords, but also fell, on this occasion when Prime Minister Boris Johnson called the 2019 General Election. The clauses have been reintroduced in Part 2 of the Judicial Review and Courts Act 2022.

The Act confers regulation-making powers on ministers to designate types of court or tribunal proceedings which are appropriate to be conducted by electronic means. Although the government stated that its intention was that the online procedure would only apply to money claims up to

[55] Lord Justice Briggs *Civil Courts Structure Review: Final Report* (July 2016), paragraph 12.6.

[56] Ministry of Justice and HMCTS *Transforming Our Justice System* (September 2016).

the value of £25,000, it also wanted ministers to have power to widen this scope in future. So the powers in the legislation cover all civil proceedings, family proceedings, and proceedings in the upper and first-tier tribunals and in employment tribunals, but not criminal proceedings.

The House of Lords Constitution Committee was concerned about the use of delegated powers to impose online proceedings for any civil claim, at any court level, which would, it said, undermine "fundamental constitutional principles", in particular the right to an oral hearing. The Committee therefore recommended that ministers should not just be required to consult with the Lord Chief Justice or the Senior President of Tribunals before exercising the powers to require or allow online hearings, but the concurrence of those judicial office-holders should be required for the exercise of the powers.[57] The government accepted that amendment at Report Stage in the House of Lords in 2019,[58] and the limitation was carried over into the 2022 Act.[59]

During the Committee Stage debates on the 2019 Bill, the minister, Lord Keen, the Advocate-General for Scotland, told the House of Lords that although "in the first instance" the online procedure would apply only to civil money claims up to the value of £25,000, "over time we of course want to widen the procedure's scope so that it covers

57 Report of the Constitution Committee of the House of Lords *Courts and Tribunals (Online Procedure) Bill* (HL Paper 373, 7 June 2019), paragraphs 8–13. I declare an interest as a member of the committee at that time.

58 *Hansard*, House of Lords, 24 June 2019, volume 798, columns 954–967.

59 Sections 19–33 of the Judicial Review and Courts Act 2022.

the civil procedures, potentially including family and tribunal proceedings".[60]

I strongly support the use of online courts for many of the reasons given by Professor Susskind and by Lord Briggs. Technology offers great opportunities for improving access to justice. But I have two main concerns. The first is pragmatic: whether the £25,000 figure (proposed by Lord Briggs, but not by Professor Susskind) is too high. I would much prefer that any move towards online courts is subject to rigorous testing in the first instance of a much smaller proportion of cases, perhaps those valued at up to £5,000 or up to £10,000. We all know from experience of government computer projects that much can go wrong. To begin with claims of up to £25,000 without extensive prior testing is, I fear, too ambitious and may well set back, rather than advance, the programme for online courts.

My second concern is one of principle: online courts should not remove the right of clients to choose that their case is presented by way of oral advocacy by their counsel. As an advocate by profession, I naturally recoil from Professor Susskind's suggestion that my function is to be "eliminated" (subject to exceptions) because clients "do not really want" me. In responding, I am mindful of what Franz Kafka said in *The Trial*, a work which has often in my career seemed more appropriate to be classified under the heading non-fiction. "The advocates", said Kafka, "had absolutely no wish to introduce or push through improvements."[61] But

[60] *Hansard*, House of Lords, 10 June 2019, volume 798, column 311.

[61] Franz Kafka *The Trial* (translated by Idris Parry, 2015), p. 96.

I shall try, as objectively as I can, to explain why I think Professor Susskind is wrong both in what he believes should happen to advocacy and in what he predicts will happen. I believe that the online court will remain the exception, confined to low-value claims, rather than the rule, and that the day in court – that is, a live physical hearing – will and should remain the standard feature of civil litigation, unless the parties agree otherwise, and also of criminal trials for at least the working lifetimes of all those starting in practice as lawyers today.

Let me seek to identify what I think is, or should be, common ground. Courts should facilitate the filing of, and access to, documents by electronic means. The law does and should encourage negotiation and mediation to limit the number of disputes which come to court. In the cases that cannot be so resolved, if the parties agree to a speedy and efficient online determination of a civil dispute without an oral hearing, I can see no reason why the law should disagree (save perhaps if the case raises issues of public importance). It may be that a large proportion of litigants will prefer, or at least accept, such procedures.

But Professor Susskind – at least in the strong version of his thesis – is not proposing voluntary new systems. His position is that in those cases where online procedures are considered suitable, their use should be "mandatory", with "no choice for the parties".[62] Or he might be content with a presumption of an online court hearing, with the parties having the opportunity (presumably in writing) to seek to

[62] Richard Susskind *Online Courts and the Future of Justice* (2019), p. 188.

persuade a judge at a case management hearing that a live hearing is more appropriate for their case.

Of course, if one of the parties prefers to have her case argued by counsel in the traditional way, that does suggest that Professor Susskind is wrong to say of that client that she "does not really want" an advocate, and that she cares only about the result. Professor Susskind responds that "[i]nexpert consumers, crudely speaking, may not know what is best for them",[63] an approach which does not explain why more expert consumers who are capable of deciding what is in their interests are also to be denied the assistance of an advocate.

In any event, the litigant may have perfectly understandable reasons for wanting a traditional hearing in which her case is presented by an advocate. She may wish to give oral evidence in a civil case which turns on an issue of fact or a question of credibility. Or she may take the view that her prospects of success are improved if her counsel is allowed to make oral submissions to explain her position to the judge.

The law should continue to accommodate such a preference. And that is because of the value of oral advocacy in assisting the court to come to a just decision and because of the social value of a court hearing in assisting litigants to see that justice has been done and so encouraging them to accept the result even though they have lost. A further concern – though I accept it may have little weight – is that if all, or most, cases involving claims for less than £25,000 are argued

[63] Richard Susskind *Online Courts and the Future of Justice* (2019), p. 51.

only in writing, young advocates are not going to gain the experience which will qualify them for arguing cases in which oral advocacy is allowed.

In a High Court case in 1968, counsel referred Mr Justice Megarry to a passage in a textbook written by the judge. His Lordship was unimpressed. He said that "argued law is tough law" and cited with approval the decision of Mr Justice Hankford in 1409 in Norman French, supplying this translation: "Today, as of old, by good disputing shall the law be well known."[64] My experience, and that of most lawyers and judges with whom I have discussed the issue, is that oral advocacy of the focused nature now customary in our courts, informed by the advance preparation which the judge carries out, is an effective means by which the court identifies the issues and tests the arguments. Judges, and I suspect juries, benefit – not always but often enough – from the competing arguments which they hear, in forming their conclusions.

Lord Justice Laws put the point clearly in a Court of Appeal judgment in 2002. He spoke of "the central place accorded to oral argument in our common law adversarial system". He recognised that "oral argument is perhaps the most powerful force there is, in our legal process, to promote a change of mind by a judge". He emphasised that to suggest that "judges in fact change their minds under the influence of oral argument is not an arcane feature of the system; it is at the centre of it". Lord Justice Keene added that oral argument

[64] *Cordell* v *Second Clanfield Properties Limited* [1969] 2 Ch 9, 16–17.

"is a process which as a matter of common experience can be markedly more effective than written argument".[65]

Oral argument gives life to the written pleadings, identifying the crucial issues and highlighting the strengths and weaknesses of the competing contentions. It gives the judge the chance to alert the advocates to whatever difficulties the court has with the position adopted by each side, and it gives the advocates an opportunity to address judicial concerns or misunderstandings.[66] Professor Dame Hazel Genn, the leading authority on the provision of civil justice, told the House of Lords Constitution Committee in 2020 that her research showed that, from a claimant's point of view, "if you go to a tribunal and you opt for a paper hearing, your chances of succeeding are much lower than if you attend the hearing physically". The research does not – yet – establish why this is so.[67]

[65] *Sengupta* v *Holmes* [2002] EWCA Civ 1104, paragraphs 38 and 47. See also *Leave.EU Group Ltd* v *Information Commissioner* [2022] 1 WLR 1909 where the Court of Appeal dismissed an appeal, without considering the substance of the issues raised, because the appellant failed to appear by lawyers or otherwise. Sir Geoffrey Vos MR, for the court, said at paragraph 20 that it would have been "undesirable . . . to try to decide such important questions at the level of the Court of Appeal without full oral argument. We have had the benefit of high quality skeleton arguments but it is extremely useful for the court in an appeal of this complexity to hear oral argument from both sides. That is particularly so when important legal issues are in play which may affect many others in society".

[66] See the Report of the Advocates' Society in Canada, *The Right to be Heard: The Future of Advocacy in Canada* (June 2021), p. 22.

[67] *Covid-19 and the Courts*, Report of the Constitution Committee of the House of Lords (HL Paper 257, 30 March 2021), paragraphs 283 and 286; and the evidence of Professor Dame Hazel Genn to the Constitution

Of course, much depends on the case, the judge and indeed the advocate making the submissions. In 2011, the Judicial Committee of the Privy Council allowed the appeal of a defendant convicted of murder in Jamaica because the incompetence of his counsel meant that he had not had a fair trial. Counsel, "on arriving late back in court following an adjournment, excused himself by saying that he had 'taken on more than I can chew'".[68] Allowing for such exceptions, what Lord Justice Laws and Lord Justice Keene said about the value of oral advocacy expresses the theory and practice of our legal system.

In any event, even when oral advocacy provides limited assistance to the court, the legal system has recognised the importance to the rule of law, and respect for it, of the right to be heard.[69] People are much more likely to accept adverse decisions if they can hear and see that the judgment follows from their representative having had a proper opportunity to put their case to the judge or jury in a physical courtroom, and they can see and hear that the court has engaged with the issues.[70]

Committee, 3 June 2020, in answer to Q24. Professor Genn said that the claimant's improved prospect of success at a physical hearing "has been known for a very long time, but the question is why? Is it because the judge can see the whites of your eyes, or is it because at a physical hearing the judge can gather information that was not available in the papers?" See also the studies referred to in the Report of the Advocates' Society in Canada, *The Right to Be Heard: The Future of Advocacy in Canada* (June 2021), p. 23.

68 *Campbell* v *The Queen* [2011] 2 AC 79, paragraph 41.

69 See Chapter 2 at nn. 36–39.

70 See the Report of the Advocates' Society in Canada, *The Right to Be Heard: The Future of Advocacy in Canada* (June 2021), p. 22: oral

When the House of Lords Constitution Committee reported in 2021 on the impact of Covid-19 on the courts, it recognised that in some contexts remote hearings risked alienating litigants because they were deprived of the face-to-face contact with their lawyers and with the judge which provided the empathy and humanity necessary to maintain their confidence in the justice system.[71] All the more so if legal disputes are to be decided without any oral hearing, live or remote. The confidence of clients, and the wider public, in the courts would be undermined by a process which fails to recognise the importance of "human interaction in respect of what is typically a significant event for the litigants and others".[72]

It may be that for younger generations this will be a factor of less significance since they are more accustomed to living so much of their lives online, but I doubt it. Judicial decisions will continue to require the payment of money, restrictions on liberty (by injunctions), or (in criminal cases) imprisonment, all backed up by the enforcement powers of the state. I would not underestimate the significance of the

hearings enable the litigant "to observe the attention and consideration being given to their case. Therefore parties may be more likely to feel heard and fairly treated if they receive the benefit of an oral hearing as opposed to a written hearing, and if they know that they (or their representative) have had the opportunity to speak directly to the decision-maker".

[71] *Covid-19 and the Courts*, Report of the Constitution Committee of the House of Lords (HL Paper 257, 30 March 2021), paragraphs 88, 97 and 106.

[72] Report of the Advocates' Society in Canada, *The Right to Be Heard: The Future of Advocacy in Canada* (June 2021), p. 43 at paragraph 5.

oral hearing in helping to secure the willingness of the losing party, and those associated with them, to accept the adverse judgment of the court.

Richard Susskind recognises that in cases raising novel points of law, judges will, at least for the foreseeable future, continue to hear argument in the traditional manner. But, he points out, such cases are "atypical"[73] and he says it is disproportionate to retain oral advocacy for standard cases which could be decided by more efficient methods which promote access to justice.

The difficulty with that approach is that a standard case, even if it does not raise an issue of law, may turn on questions of credibility, and in any event it may be of considerable importance to the litigant – either financially or personally – for all sorts of reasons depending on their individual circumstances. I do not accept that the law should, in the interests of promoting access to courts generally, tell the litigant that she does not have the right to have her case presented by an advocate, if she wishes, before she is ordered to pay what may be for her a substantial sum of money to the other party, or is made subject to an injunction. The current policy proposal (based on the recommendation of Lord Briggs) is for at least a presumption of online assessment where claims are for less than £25,000. That is a very large sum of money for most people, and in any event, as Richard Susskind acknowledges, "[a] low-value case can raise highly sensitive personal issues which might best be handled in

[73] Richard Susskind *Online Courts and the Future of Justice* (2019), p. 44.

person. A low-value case can also raise very challenging legal questions".[74]

All the more so if the case raises issues of family law, or public law, for example – add your own area of expertise – or if a criminal charge is brought. In all such sensitive cases, I think people who are litigating, whether as claimant or defendant, value the opportunity to have their advocate voice their grievance, their response, their apology, and would be much less likely to accept an adverse decision if they have not seen the judge listen to the argument before giving judgment. The losing party who was denied an oral hearing will be much more likely to take up legal resources by seeking to appeal.

Article 6 of the European Convention on Human Rights, incorporated into domestic law by the Human Rights Act 1998, guarantees the right to a fair hearing. The European Court of Human Rights has interpreted this to confer on a party to civil or criminal litigation a right to an oral hearing in a court of first instance, unless there are exceptional circumstances that justify dispensing with such a procedure.[75] The European Court has accepted that an oral hearing is not required if a civil dispute raises "no questions of fact or law which cannot be adequately resolved" by a written procedure.[76]

[74] Richard Susskind *Online Courts and the Future of Justice* (updated paperback edition, 2021), p. xxxi.

[75] See, for example, the decisions of the European Court of Human Rights in *Hakansson and Sturesson* v *Sweden* (1990) 13 EHRR 1, at paragraph 64; *Fischer* v *Austria* (1995) 20 EHRR 349, at paragraph 44; and *Goc* v *Turkey* (Grand Chamber, 11 July 2002) at paragraph 47.

[76] *Pursiheimo* v *Finland* (2003) 38 EHRR CD 138, 142 (European Court of Human Rights).

Or if the issues are technical in nature, as in social security law.[77] The European Court has emphasised that the test is not dependent on the "frequency" of such cases but on the nature of the issues for resolution.[78] Nevertheless, to adopt at least a presumption that there is no right to an oral hearing in civil litigation would be to turn the Article 6 principle on its head. I do not see how the right to an oral hearing could be removed as the standard means by which the court decides civil or indeed criminal cases without a breach of Article 6 or without a radical restatement of the basic principles of that provision.[79]

Professor Susskind argues that because many people cannot afford to pay for an advocate at an oral hearing of a civil claim, and the state cannot or will not pay for them to receive such assistance, the result is "significant distributive injustice", especially if the ability to pay for an advocate confers a litigation advantage.[80] This is an argument not accepted – yet – in relation to other services of vital importance to the public: we can choose to pay for a private education for our children, and for private medical insurance for ourselves and our family, if we believe it confers a benefit, even though there are many people who cannot afford to

[77] *Miller* v *Sweden* (European Court of Human Rights, 8 February 2005), paragraph 29.

[78] *Saccoccia* v *Austria* (European Court of Human Rights, 18 December 2008), paragraphs 73–74.

[79] The use of a video link is not, as such, inconsistent with Article 6: *R (Michael)* v *Governor of Whitemoor Prison* [2020] 1 WLR 2524 (Lord Burnett, Chief Justice, for the Court of Appeal).

[80] Richard Susskind *Online Courts and the Future of Justice* (2019), pp. 232–233.

exercise such a choice and even though buying the benefit may give those with greater financial resources a significant advantage – indeed, it might on occasions be a life-saving advantage. Rather than abolish the right of the well-off to pay for such benefits, the state seeks to focus on improving the general provision of publicly funded education and healthcare for all. I see no reason why a different approach should be adopted in relation to access to legal services.[81]

That is also part of the answer to those who say that it is wrong that wealthy people should be able to pay for expensive counsel, perhaps a KC, when the other side to the litigation can only afford a cheaper advocate (or cannot afford to pay for any advocate). The litigant has a right to competent representation, not to the best representation that (he or she thinks) money can buy. In 2002, two men convicted of robbery appealed to the Court of Appeal against their conviction on the ground that the prosecution case had been presented by a Queen's Counsel but they were only represented, at

[81] Richard Susskind is entitled to say, and does say, to lawyers: well what would *you* do to enhance access to the courts if you are not going to promote online determination of disputes: *Online Courts and the Future of Justice* (2019), p. 184. My response is that we should do all we can to make court proceedings as intelligible to litigants as possible; we should encourage mediation and other means of settlement of disputes; we should seek to persuade government to improve both the scope of civil legal aid and the value of payments made; and we should encourage the market to develop new forms of litigation funding. What we should not do in response to concerns about access to the courts is remove the right of the litigant to have her case argued at a hearing by a professional advocate if the issue is of sufficient importance to her that she rejects online resolution.

public expense, by junior counsel (that is, a barrister who is not a QC). Lord Woolf, for the Court of Appeal, accepted that the principle of equality of arms is part of the common law, as well as guaranteed by the Human Rights Act 1998. But, he concluded, a fair trial does not require that the defendant be represented by a QC simply because the prosecution is so represented: what is important "is to have an advocate, whether he be a barrister or a solicitor, who can ensure that a defendant's defence is properly and adequately placed before the court".[82]

Indeed, an expensive lawyer is not necessarily the best lawyer, or even a good lawyer. There are many highly competent advocates from which to choose. The Bar is now a very competitive market. If a litigant is represented by inadequate counsel, or is unrepresented, judges do all they can to protect the litigant's interests.

During the debates on the Courts and Tribunals (Online Procedure) Bill 2019, Lord Keen, speaking for the government, assured the House of Lords that he was "not aware of any proposal to attempt to replicate the ability of our judiciary with artificial intelligence".[83] Richard Susskind recognises that there is, as yet, no computer programme "that can generate legal argument".[84] But he says that a "second generation" of online courts "can in principle be envisaged"

[82] *Attorney-General's Reference(No. 82a of 2000), R* v *Lea and R* v *Shatwell* [2002] 2 Cr App R 342, 345, paragraph 14.

[83] *Hansard*, House of Lords, 14 May 2019, column 1524 (Second Reading).

[84] Richard Susskind *Online Courts and the Future of Justice* (2019), p. 156: "we are not there yet; not by a long way".

where "determinations will be made by some form of artificial intelligence". He acknowledges that "[t]oday this may seem outrageous", although he suggests that "within two decades or so, the use of [artificial intelligence] may well be commonplace for appropriate cases".[85] In October 2020, an AI expert predicted that within fifty years, "robot judges" would be deciding "with 99.9 per cent accuracy" whether a witness giving evidence in a criminal or civil case is telling the truth by assessing speech patterns, increases in body temperature and eye movement.[86]

Perhaps. In around 1682, the philosopher Gottfried Leibniz aimed to produce a machine to assist in "the analysis of truth". So two persons debating would be able to say to each other, "Let us calculate", and thereby determine who is correct.[87] Jonathan Swift parodied Leibniz's ideas in *Gulliver's Travels*. Gulliver visits the Grand Academy of Lagado, where a professor shows him a machine consisting of large numbers of pieces of wood linked together by wires, to which are attached papers containing "all the words of their language in their several moods, tenses and declensions". The professor's pupils turn the machine with the aid of iron handles, altering the order of the words. The results are recorded in the hope that books may be written in "philosophy, poetry, laws, mathematics and theology without the least assistance from genius or study". Swift added, a little unfairly – but since

[85] Richard Susskind *Online Courts and the Future of Justice* (2019), p. 117.

[86] *Mail Online* 20 October 2020 reporting the views of Terence Mauri.

[87] G W Leibniz *The Art of Controversies* (translated and edited by Marcelo Dascal, 2008), pp. 216–217.

when was parody subject to judicial review for fairness – that the Lagado Academy was also studying ways of producing food from human excrement.[88]

We are, as Professor Susskind acknowledges, nowhere near being able to create a machine which, by the application of algorithms to the written representations of both sides, produces a judgment, far less a reasoned judgment, even in easy cases where there are no complex questions of law.[89] In any event, the result would inevitably depend on the content of the algorithms which the computer would apply – algorithms that may be infected, however unintentionally, by the bias or judgment of the computer programmer. Even more difficult would be the task of enabling a computer to exercise the discretion which the judge applies in many areas of the law: whether to grant an injunction, or remove a child into care, or decide on the length of a sentence for a crime in the light of all the circumstances of the case.

Even if decisions of that nature were to become within the technological capability of a computer, I am doubtful that future generations of losing parties would be willing to trust the "judgment" of a computer on such matters. Such judgments would not command the respect that is so vital to the rule of law – unless human nature develops as radically as the technology. As human beings, we see intrinsic value in

[88] Jonathan Swift *Gulliver's Travels* (1726), "A Voyage to Laputa etc", chapter 5.

[89] Richard Susskind *Online Courts and the Future of Justice* (2019), pp. 280–281.

decisions being taken by other human beings, whose decisions we can seek to influence and whose reasoning we can, if necessary, criticise and challenge, even if the process may be inefficient. Confidence in computers is also undermined by events such as the scandal of the wrongful convictions of Post Office employees for offences of dishonesty when the accounting discrepancies were in fact caused by the malfunctioning Horizon computer system, leading to the Court of Appeal quashing the convictions of dozens of postmasters in April 2021.[90] I would also not underestimate the human fear that a technically sophisticated machine, like the errant computer HAL in Stanley Kubrick's 1968 film *2001: A Space Odyssey*, may develop an agenda of its own.

If judgments *were* ever to be delivered by a computer, the advocate would then be redundant. It would be futile for counsel to make oral submissions to a judicial machine devoid of human empathy. Let us call it Diplock. There would be no point doing so because Diplock would already appreciate the strength and weaknesses of all the arguments in the light of the data to which it has access. Oral advocacy from a human being could not assist. The oracle will have spoken – though there will still be disputes about what the oracle's statement means, as in cases where domestic courts tried to understand Delphic utterances from the Court of Justice of the EU in Luxembourg. The question also arises that if artificial intelligence were ever able to decide legal disputes, why should we confine Diplock to deciding such matters? Why

[90] *Hamilton* v *Post Office Limited* [2021] EWCA Crim 577.

not also business decisions, or political disputes? Indeed why leave any important decision to human beings?

This is not a factor which should affect the decision of a student whether now to come to the Bar, not least because if computer technology were to develop more radically than I believe to be likely or acceptable, that would affect all professions, not just advocacy.

I turn to the third challenge to the future of advocacy: will bright young students still wish to pursue a career as an advocate, which normally means coming to the Bar either at the beginning of your career or at some later stage, though there are solicitors who specialise in advocacy.

There are many challenges which the young barrister faces. In particular, first, the difficulty of finding pupillage and then a tenancy in Chambers. Second, the uncertainty of whether they will then find work, and whether it will be sufficiently well remunerated. Talented young lawyers know that they can earn large salaries from solicitors' firms from the day they join. They know that their early years at the Bar, and sometimes the years after that, will involve greater risks, especially with the severe reductions in the scope and amount of legal aid.[91]

[91] See "Barristers quit over low pay and delays" *The Times* 18 October 2021: research by the Criminal Bar Association found that 22 per cent of junior members of the criminal Bar have left the profession since 2016. In April 2022, the Criminal Bar Association encouraged its members to "work to rule" by not accepting cases from other barristers who were due to appear but could no longer do so because another of their cases had overrun. Bar leaders took that action because poor pay on legal aid cases had resulted in "increasing numbers . . . leaving our ranks to find

The Bar has made great efforts over the past twenty years to promote diversity in its ranks. Its future depends on young lawyers from all backgrounds taking the risk and joining the profession. I want to encourage them to do so. I hope that young lawyers will not be deterred by the challenges, when the potential rewards, both in financial terms[92] in some areas of the law, and in terms of job satisfaction, can be substantial.

Even for a large financial reward, you may not wish to sit in a city solicitor's office drafting commercial contracts or checking what documents need to be disclosed. And perhaps sit there from early morning until very late at night: according to a survey published in October 2021, trainees employed by the US law firm Kirkland & Ellis on average start work at 9.14am and finish at 11.28pm, and many other leading firms have an average finish time after 9pm.[93]

Instead, you can have, from your first weeks in practice at the Bar after pupillage, responsibility for arguing a case. What advice do you give your client in the immigration tribunal in relation to her asylum claim? Who do you call as a witness in the employment tribunal in your client's claim

alternative work that offers a viable career". They said that over the past two decades, real incomes for criminal defence advocates had declined by 28 per cent. See *The Times* 11 April 2022. Unhappiness about low pay for some lawyers is not confined to the United Kingdom. See "Lawyer is happier and better paid after quitting her job to become a pet psychic": *American Bar Association Journal*, posted 9 June 2022 referring to an article in the *New York Post* 7 June 2022.

[92] See nn. 96–104 below.

[93] *Legal Cheek*, published on 26 October 2021.

for unfair dismissal? What questions do you put in cross-examination? How do you deal with the hostile, or indeed the sympathetic, judge?

The conduct of the case is the responsibility of the advocate.[94] Therefore, said the Lord Chief Justice, Lord Thomas of Cwmgiedd, for the Court of Appeal in 2015, there is "no basis upon which an advocate can be instructed as to what to say in his closing speech by his solicitor or by his client or when to conclude it. That is the advocate's responsibility".[95] And what a responsibility it is. The young lawyer conducting a case in an employment tribunal, like the more experienced lawyer appearing in the Supreme Court, has the challenges and the opportunities it presents.

The potential financial earnings for successful barristers are high, though not as much as was received by Sir Robert Heath, the Attorney-General, in the 1620s. He "was given the entire province of Carolina, together with the Bahamas, as a reward for exceptional services in 1628–1629".[96] There is no rule of professional practice requiring counsel to act on the advice of Quintilian that "[t]he orator will not seek to make

[94] *R* v *Farooqi* [2014] 1 Crim App R 9, paragraphs 107–109 (Lord Chief Justice Judge for the Court of Appeal).

[95] *R* v *Ekaireb* [2015] EWCA Crim 1936, paragraph 6. The Court of Appeal noted at paragraph 52 that the speech given by defence counsel at the trial of his client, who was convicted of murder, was "ill-judged, patronising and contained inappropriate attempts at humour", but nevertheless "it did not reach a level of incompetence that called into question the fairness of the trial or safety of the conviction".

[96] Sir John Baker *An Introduction to English Legal History* (2019), p. 175, n. 45.

more money than he needs".[97] F. Lee Bailey – a very prominent US advocate until he was disbarred from practice in Florida in 2001 for misconduct – commented that he had "knowingly defended a number of guilty men. But the guilty never escape unscathed. My fees are sufficient punishment for anyone".[98] Legal fees have long been a subject of fascination. In *Romeo and Juliet*, Shakespeare suggests that lawyers "straight dream on fees".[99] Bertie Wooster commented, after some out-of-court advocacy by him, that "[i]t was the sort of thing you have to pay topnotchers at the Bar a king's ransom for".[100]

Barristers can be very well paid because their fees are often not based on hours worked. Justice Woolsey explained for the US District Court in 1930 that "[t]he value of a lawyer's services is not measured by time or labour merely. The practice of law is an art in which success depends as much as in any other art on the application of imagination – and sometimes inspiration – to the subject-matter".[101] Mr Justice Walton similarly noted in a 1978 case that, for the professional, "[i]deas – often very valuable ideas – occur in the train or car home, or in the bath, or even whilst watching television".[102] This principle has limits. In 2015, lawyer Yarboro Sallee was suspended by the Tennessee Supreme Court for one

[97] Quintilian *The Orator's Education*, Book 12, chapter 7 (edited and translated by Donald A Russell, 2001), p. 263.

[98] *Oxford Dictionary of American Legal Quotations* (edited by Fred R Shapiro, 1993), p. 142.

[99] Act 1, Scene 4.

[100] P G Wodehouse *Much Obliged Jeeves* (1971), chapter 15.

[101] *Woodbury* v *Andrew Jergens Co* 37 F Supp 749, 750 (1930).

[102] *Maltby* v *D J Freeman & Co* [1978] 1 WLR 431, 435.

year for ethical violations which included billing clients for the time spent watching true-crime shows on television as "research" for representing their interests.[103] And Kristin Ann Stahlbush was suspended from practice by the Ohio Supreme Court in 2010 for two years for overbilling for work done by claiming for more than twenty-four hours a day.[104]

In *King Lear*, the Fool refers to "the breath of an unfee'd lawyer" and Lear responds that "nothing can be made out of nothing".[105] If that were ever true, it certainly is not today when many barristers devote substantial time to acting pro bono (that is for no fee) for clients who cannot afford to pay, and have no access to legal aid.

At the beginning of the nineteenth century, the future Lord Chancellor Henry Brougham believed, at the age of twenty-one, that practice at the English bar was "tedious", involving work "among a set of disagreeable people of brutal manners and confined talents".[106] In a long career at the Bar,

[103] *American Bar Association Journal*, posted 13 August 2015.

[104] *Toledo Bar Association* v *Stahlbush* (Ohio Supreme Court, 24 August 2010). Cf the "modesty of the fees" charged by Alexander Hamilton: Chapter 2 at n. 23.

[105] Act 1, Scene 4.

[106] R E Megarry *A New Miscellany-at-Law* (edited by Bryan A Garner, 2005), pp. 11–12. See also Sir William Blackstone *Commentaries on the Laws of England* (1765), volume 1, p. 33: "we must rarely expect to see a gentleman of distinction or learning at the bar". Lord Hoffmann asked Professor Herbert Hart "why he did not return after the war to his successful practice at the Chancery Bar and he said he found it too trivial": *Memorial Addresses of All Souls College, Oxford* (edited by Peregrine Horden, 2022), p. 280: Lord Hoffmann's Memorial Address for Michael Hart.

I have been fortunate to enjoy a more satisfying working life. I have had a front-row seat in court to watch drama, tragedy, and sometimes farce. I have met extraordinary people – clients from all walks of life, judges, solicitors, colleagues and opponents.

There is no normal day for a barrister. After losing a case in the Appellate Committee of the House of Lords, I have been asked to give written advice on whether it was possible to sue the presiding Lord of Appeal, Lord Keith of Kinkel, for negligence. I have spent two days in the Court of Appeal arguing about "the meaning of the words 'is' and 'where'".[107] I have made submissions to the Video Appeals Tribunal sitting in Soho about how close a close-up is acceptable in the video films *Horny Catbabe* and *Nympho Nurse Nancy*, classified as suitable to be sold only in a licensed sex shop.[108] I have been instructed by a mother who had taken her children abroad to tell the family court judge that he could make any order he liked, but my client had no intention of complying with it. I have attempted, in a sports tribunal, to cross-examine in English a witness who claimed only to speak Swahili. During the Covid-19 pandemic, I have sat at my desk in chambers at 2 o'clock in the morning, dressed in my wig

107 *Royal Mail Group plc* v *Consumer Council for Postal Services* [2007] EWCA Civ 167, paragraph 58 (Sedley LJ for the Court of Appeal). As Sedley LJ there observed, this "might be thought either an indictment or a vindication of our system of oral advocacy".

108 *Sheptonhurst Ltd* v *British Board of Film Classification* (Video Appeals Committee, 16 August 1999). This was not Gloria Swanson as Norma Desmond delivering her line in *Sunset Boulevard* – "I'm ready for my close-up Mr de Mille".

and gown, arguing a case remotely in the Hong Kong Court of Final Appeal.[109] I have been told by an American client prior to a hearing in the Court of Appeal to "crap all over" the other side. Only once, I think, have I been blessed by my client – a vicar who was attempting to stop the ordination of women – as I stood up to make my submissions to the Court of Appeal.[110]

Advocates about to begin their legal careers look forward to presenting a devastating cross-examination, securing the acquittal of their client at the Old Bailey, or winning that important case in the Court of Appeal. When Thomas Erskine won a case advancing liberty at the end of the eighteenth century, "[b]onfires were lit in every part of the kingdom in his honour. . . . Portraits and busts of him were sold by the thousand; a hundred cities offered him their freedom".[111] Gustave Flaubert dedicated his 1857 novel *Madame Bovary* to his lawyer Marie-Antoine-Jules Sénard for securing his acquittal after he was prosecuted for immorality on publication of the serialised version. Flaubert wrote that he could

[109] In another Hong Kong case in which I was participating remotely from London, the Chief Justice intervened just as my submissions were warming up to tell me that he had been handed a note saying that my client (who had been brought to court from prison) needed to go to the lavatory.

[110] *Re Williamson The Times* 9 March 1994. Counsel for the Archbishops of Canterbury and York argued that the claim should be dismissed for delay by my client in starting the legal proceedings. The Master of the Rolls, Sir Thomas Bingham, said that it would be inappropriate to decide the case on such a ground, given that the issues had an eternal character. The claim was dismissed on several other grounds.

[111] Lord Birkett *Six Great Advocates* (1961), p. 82.

"never adequately repay either your eloquence or your devoted loyalty".[112] P. G. Wodehouse dedicated *Right Ho Jeeves* to Rodney Needham KC "with affection and admiration" after he won an appeal against an income tax assessment.[113]

You may dream of emulating Sir Henry Hawkins who boasted in his memoirs that as he was leaving court after succeeding for the prosecution in the perjury case against the Tichborne claimant in 1874, the presiding judge, Lord Chief Justice Cockburn, said to him "Bravo! Bravo, Hawkins!" According to Hawkins, the Lord Chief Justice added, "I have not heard a piece of oratory like that for many a long day!", and the judge "patted me cordially on the back as he looked at me with, I believe, the sincerest appreciation".[114] After the criminal libel proceedings brought by Oscar Wilde against the Marquess of Queensberry failed, Mr Justice Henn Collins wrote to Sir Edward Carson, who had acted for the Defendant, to congratulate him: "I never heard a more powerful speech or a more searching cross-examination. I congratulate you on having escaped most of the filth".[115]

You may aspire to achieve the fame of a celebrated advocate referred to in popular culture. In Ben Hecht and Charles MacArthur's 1928 play *The Front Page*, the newspaper editor, Walter Burns, shouts out, "Get Clarence

[112] Gustave Flaubert *Madame Bovary* (translated by Margaret Mauldon, 2004), pp. 3 and 312.

[113] Frances Donaldson *P G Wodehouse: A Biography* (1982), pp. 153–154.

[114] *The Reminiscences of Sir Henry Hawkins* (edited by Richard Harris KC, 1904), p. 223.

[115] H. Montgomery Hyde *Famous Trials 7* (1962), p. 149 and Richard Ellmann *Oscar Wilde* (1987), p. 425.

Darrow".[116] In an episode of the 1957 television comedy *Hancock's Half Hour*, the head of chambers complains that Hancock, an unsuccessful barrister, disgraced himself in court because he "turned up drunk and spent the entire afternoon trying to sit on Rose Heilbron's knee".[117]

I have had my share of satisfying victories. The cases of which I am most proud include appearing for gay servicemen and women who established in the European Court of Human Rights that it was a breach of their human rights for them to be dismissed from the services because of their sexual orientation.[118] I acted for Debbie Purdy, suffering from multiple sclerosis, who established in the final House of Lords appeal before the creation of the Supreme Court that the Director of Public Prosecutions, Keir Starmer QC – whatever happened to him? – was obliged to issue guidance on when he would prosecute a person who assists another to commit suicide.[119] And I acted for Gina Miller in two Brexit cases, establishing first that Prime Minister Theresa May could not lawfully notify the European Union of this country's intention to leave in 2016 without the prior approval of an Act of Parliament,[120] and then that Prime Minister Boris Johnson had unlawfully exercised prerogative powers by advising Her

[116] Ben Hecht and Charles MacArthur *The Front Page* (1955), Act III, p. 134.

[117] *The Crown* v *James (S)* broadcast on 2 December 1957, written by Alan Simpson and Ray Galton.

[118] *Lustig-Prean* v *United Kingdom* (1999) 29 EHRR 548.

[119] *R (Purdy)* v *Director of Public Prosecutions* [2010] 1 AC 345.

[120] *R (Miller)* v *Secretary of State for Exiting the European Union* [2018] AC 61.

Majesty the Queen to prorogue, that is suspend, Parliament in the autumn of 2019 in the run-up to the date then fixed for Brexit.[121] The rule of law has advanced since counsel, James Whitelocke, was prosecuted in the Star Chamber in 1613 "for a contempt of the King's Prerogative" by giving an Opinion to a client that the King's prerogative powers were limited. Whitelocke abjectly apologised and was pardoned.[122]

But like all other advocates,[123] I have also had my share of disasters, many of them still too painful to recall. My first case was in 1980 as second junior to Anthony Lester QC in the Judicial Committee of the Privy Council on an appeal from Singapore. Our client had been sentenced to death for drug trafficking. The issue of law was whether the mandatory sentence was a breach of his constitutional rights. We lost. Our client was hanged.[124] You can only improve after such a start.[125]

Rudyard Kipling went on about treating triumph and disaster just the same. He did not lose a case 17–0 in the European Court of Human Rights, a result not entirely due to my advocacy for the losing party, the United Kingdom, in 1999 in the case brought by Robert Thompson and Jon

[121] *R (Miller)* v *Prime Minister* [2020] AC 373.

[122] *Proceedings against Mr James Whitelocke* (1613) 2 State Trials 765.

[123] See Chapter 1, nn. 32–38.

[124] *Ong Ah Chuan* v *Public Prosecutor* [1981] AC 648.

[125] I have, I hope, never exhibited the arrogance described by Anne Robinson *Memoirs of an Unfit Mother* (2001), p. 3. After arguing the custody case concerning her infant daughter, and before the judge gave his decision, her QC told her, "If I say it myself, I did rather well. A lesson in advocacy for any young pupil listening". She lost.

Venables complaining that the English criminal justice system had dealt unfairly with them as ten-year-old defendants convicted of the murder of the two-year-old child James Bulger.[126] In a judicial review application, my opponent and friend Lord Grabiner QC told the Divisional Court that my submissions were wrong for "at least five reasons", and "no doubt there were a number of others but", he said, he got "bored after five". In substance, the court agreed.[127] I have suffered the indignity of my victorious clients' application that the other side pay the full costs of retaining me being rejected by Mr Justice Blake with the memorable words that this is a "court of justice not a casino".[128]

I have acted for all sorts, from Princess Diana to Robert Maxwell; from Her Majesty the Queen to asylum-seekers; from the Chief Rabbi to the Revd Moon. I have enjoyed the life of an advocate. Unfortunately I do not find any truth in the suggestion by Quintilian in his first century AD study of advocacy, that the further you go in your career, the less preparation is required, and that "the fruits offer themselves without effort . . . and all things come forth unbidden".[129] That is a recipe for disaster.

[126] *V and T* v *United Kingdom* (1999) 30 EHRR 121.

[127] *R (SRM Global Master Fund LP and others)* v *Commissioners of Her Majesty's Treasury* [2009] EWHC 227 (Admin). See the transcript of oral argument, 14 January 2009, p. 172. The Court of Appeal dismissed an appeal by my clients: [2009] EWCA Civ 788.

[128] *The Guardian* 3 March 2016. The case was *Al Attiya* v *Bin-Jassim Bin-Jaber Al Thani* [2016] EWHC 212 (QB).

[129] Quintilian *The Orator's Education*, Book 12, chapter 10 (edited and translated by Donald A Russell, 2001), p. 323.

Quintilian also suggests, more persuasively, that the advocate coming to the end of her career should retire before her skills decline. The advocate should "make for the harbour while his ship is still sound" and then "compose a treatise on oratory".[130] I am not yet ready to do so as I can still say, like Dr Huld, Joseph K's advocate in Kafka's *The Trial*, "[t]o be honest with you, I find the matter so interesting that I can't bring myself to give up this chance to participate".[131]

I hope that these Hamlyn lectures will encourage young people from all backgrounds to think of a career as an advocate, despite – indeed because of – its pressures and its challenges, and despite the uncertainties posed by technological developments. You will need the support of parents, partners and colleagues, a strong constitution, an appetite for hard work, a thick skin and a large quantity of luck. But you will have fun. As Lord Bingham told a student, "Go to the bar – that's where the magic is".[132]

130 Quintilian *The Orator's Education*, Book 12, chapter 11 (edited and translated by Donald A Russell, 2001), p. 327. Quintilian also advises, in Book 12, chapter 11, p. 325, that the advocate should know when to stop: to take care not "to become halting in his speech through fatigue, to realise that his words are no longer listened to, or to look in vain for his former self".

131 Franz Kafka *The Trial* (translated by Idris Parry, 2015), p. 81.

132 Simon Brown *Playing Off the Roof and Other Stories* (2020), p. 29.

INDEX

For EU product safety concerns, contact us at Calle de José Abascal, 56–1°, 28003 Madrid, Spain or eugpsr@cambridge.org.

www.ingramcontent.com/pod-product-compliance
Lightning Source LLC
LaVergne TN
LVHW010320220926
848484LV00004BB/810

* 9 7 8 1 0 0 9 3 3 8 1 0 3 *